Reveling

THROUGH

REVELATION

Part 1 — Chapters 1-11

by

J. VERNON McGEE, Th.D., LL.D.

THRU THE BIBLE BOOKS
Box 100
Pasadena, California 91109

First Printing, May 1962
Sixth Printing, September 1974
Seventh Printing, September 1979
Eighth Printing, December 1979

FOREWORD

These notes and outlines were first mimeographed for the Thursday night Bible Study at the Church of the Open Door in Los Angeles.

Later they were used on the Hi Noon radio broadcast and other broadcasts which I have conducted. Many have placed the mimeographed copies in notebooks that they might be available for further study.

The purpose for this publication of the notes is to put them in a more permanent form, and to provide access for more folk who want to make a detailed study of the Revelation.

To aid the student of Scripture in this enterprise, the Authorized version is given so that there will not be the necessity of referring back and forth from the Bible to the notes. In addition, a translation of mine is given in *italicized* type where there is a need to clear up the meaning of the Author or to simplify the text.

This is a word-by-word study, rather than a verse-by-verse study. The verses are man made, but God gave the Word.

This is another volume in a series of notes which we have prepared on the different books of the Bible.

We send these forth with the prayer that they may prove practical for the average Christian as he seeks to study God's holy Word.

INTRODUCTION

When the Pilgrims sailed for America, their pastor at Leyden reminded them, "The Lord has more truth yet to break forth from His Holy Word . . . . Luther and Calvin were great shining lights in their times, yet they penetrated not the whole counsel of God. . . . Be ready to receive whatever truth shall be made known to you from the written word of God." The 20th century has witnessed a renewed interest in eschatology (doctrine of last things), especially since World War I. Great strides have been made in the field of prophecy during the past two decades. Indeed new light has fallen upon this phase of Scripture. All of this attention has focused the light of deeper study on the book of Revelation.

In these brief notes we shall avoid the pitfalls of attempting to present something new and novel just for the sake of being different. Likewise, we shall steer clear of repeating threadbare cliches. Many works on Revelation are merely a carbon copy of other works.

By notes, comments, remarks, diagrams and word studies we shall attempt to get at the real meaning of the vision and symbols of Revelation.

There have been many approaches to this book, but these can be divided into four major systems. (Broadus lists 7 theories of interpretation, Tregelles lists 3.)

1. **Preterest Theory.** All of Revelation has been fulfilled in the past. It had to do with local references in John's day. It had to do with the days of either Nero or Domitian. This view was held by Renan and most German scholars, also by Elliott.

2. **Historical Theory.** Fulfillment of Revelation is going on in history, and Revelation is the prophetic history of the church, according to this theory.

3. **Historical-Spiritual Theory** is a refinement of the historical theory which was advanced by Sir William Ramsey. This theory states that the two beasts are Imperial and Provincial Rome. The point of the book is to encourage Christians. According to this theory, Revelation has been largely fulfilled and there are spiritual lessons for the church today. Amillennialism for the most part, has adopted this view. It dissipates and defeats the purpose of the book.

4. **Futurist Theory** holds that the book of Revelation is primarily prophetic and yet future, especially from Revelation 4 on to the end of the book. This is the view of all pre-millennialists and is the view which we accept and present.

SIX STRIKING AND SINGULAR FEATURES

1. It is the only prophetic book in the New Testament (in contrast to 17 prophetic books in the Old Testament).
2. John, the writer, reaches farther back into eternity past than any other writer in Scripture (John 1:1-3). He reaches farther on into eternity future in the book of Revelation.

3

3. Special blessing is promised the readers of this book (Revelation 1:3). Likewise, a warning is issued to those who tamper with its contents (Revelation 22:18, 19).

4. Revelation is not a sealed book (Revelation 22:10). Contrast Daniel 12:9. It is a revelation (apocalypse), which is an unveiling.

5. It is a series of visions, expressed in symbols.

6. This book is like a great union station where the great trunk lines of prophecy come in from other portions of Scripture. Revelation does not originate but consumates. It is imperative to a right understanding of the book to be able to trace each great subject of prophecy from the first reference to the terminal. There are at least 10 great subjects of prophecy which find their consummation here:

(1) The Lord Jesus Christ (Genesis 3:15).

(2) The Church (Matthew 16:18).

(3) The Resurrection and Translation of Saints (I Thes. 4:13-18; I Cor. 15:51, 52).

(4) The Great Tribulation (Deuteronomy 4:30, 31).

(5) Satan and Evil (Ezekiel 28:11-18).

(6) The "Man of Sin" (Ezekiel 28:1-10).

(7) The Course and End of Apostate Christendom (Daniel 2:31-45; Matthew 13).

(8) The Beginning, Course, and End of the "Times of the Gentiles" (Daniel 2:37; Luke 21:24).

(9) The Second Coming of Christ (Jude 14, 15).

(10) Israel's Covenants (Genesis 12:1-3), five things promised Israel.

REVELATION—APOCALYPSE

Key: Revelation 1:18-19

"Alpha—Omega"   "Things . . . seen"   "Beginning—End"

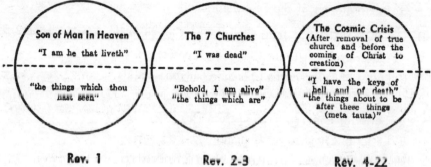

PAST	PRESENT	FUTURE
Son of Man In Heaven "I am he that liveth" "the things which thou hast seen"	The 7 Churches "I was dead" "Behold, I am alive" "the things which are"	The Cosmic Crisis (After removal of true church and before the coming of Christ to creation) "I have the keys of hell and of death" "the things about to be after these things (meta tauta)"
Rev. 1	Rev. 2-3	Rev. 4-22
Christ in Glory	Church in the World	Crisis in the Future

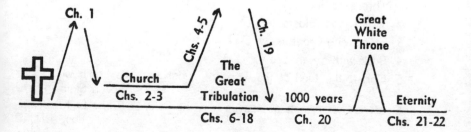

Ch. 1

Chs. 4-5

Ch. 19

Great
White
Throne

Church
Chs. 2-3

The
Great
Tribulation
Chs. 6-18

1000 years
Ch. 20

Eternity
Chs. 21-22

OUTLINE

I. The PERSON of Jesus Christ—Christ in Glory, chapter 1

A. Title of the Book, verse 1

B. Method of Revelation, verse 2

C. Beatitude of Bible Study, verse 3

D. Greetings from John the Writer, and from Jesus Christ in Heaven, verses 4-8

E. The Post-Incarnate Christ in a Glorified Body, Judging His Church (the Great High Priest in the Holy of Holies), verses 9-18 *"we know him no longer after the flesh"*

F. Time Division of the Contents of the Apocalypse, verse 19

G. Interpretation of the Seven Stars and Seven Lampstands, verse 20

II. The POSSESSION of Jesus Christ—The Church in the World, chaps. 2, 3

A. Letter of Christ to the Church in Ephesus, 2:1-7

B. Letter of Christ to the Church in Smyrna, 2:8-11

C. Letter of Christ to the Church in Pergamum, 2:12-17

D. Letter of Christ to the Church in Thyatira, 2:18-29

E. Letter of Christ to the Church in Sardis, 3:1-6

F. Letter of Christ to the Church in Philadelphia, 3:7-13

G. Letter of Christ to the Church in Laodicea, 3:14-22

III. The PROGRAM of Jesus Christ—The Scene in Heaven, chapters 4-22

A. The Church in Heaven with Christ, chapters 4-5

"I will come again, and receive you unto myself; that where I am, there ye may be also"

1. Throne of God, 4:1-3

2. Twenty-four Elders, 4:4, 5

3. Four Living Creatures, 4:6-11

4. Book with Seven Seals, 5:1-4

5. Christ: the Lion of the Tribe of Judah and the Lamb which Has Been Slain, 5:5-10

6. Myriads of Angels of Heaven Join the Song of Praise and Redemption, 5:11, 12

7. Universal Worship of the Saviour and Sovereign of the Universe, 5:13, 14

B. The Great Tribulation in the World, chapters 6-18

1. Opening of the **Seven-Sealed Book,** chapters 6-8:1
   a. Opening of the First Seal, 6:1, 2
      (Rider on a White Horse)
   b. Opening of the Second Seal, 6:3, 4
      (Rider on a Red Horse)
   c. Opening of the Third Seal, 6:5, 6
      (Rider on a Black Horse)
   d. Opening of the Fourth Seal, 6:7, 8
      (Rider on a Pale Horse)
   e. Opening of the Fifth Seal, 6:9-11
      (Prayer of the Martyred Remnant)
   f. Opening of the Sixth Seal, 6:12-17
      (The Day of Wrath Has Come—Beginning the Last Half of the Great Tribulation)
   g. Interlude, chapter 7
      (1). Reason for the Interlude Between the 6th and 7th Seals, 7:1-3
      (2). Remnant of Israel Sealed, 7:4-8
      (3). Redeemed Multitude of Gentiles, 7:9-17
   h. Opening of the Seventh Seal—Introduction of Seven Trumpets, 8:1

2. Blowing of the **Seven Trumpets,** chapters 8:2-11:19
   a. Angel at the Altar with Censer of Incense, 8:2-6
   b. First Trumpet—Trees Burnt, 8:7
   c. Second Trumpet—Seas Become Blood, 8:8, 9
   d. Third Trumpet—Fresh Water Becomes Bitter, 8:10, 11
   e. Fourth Trumpet—Sun, Moon, Stars Smitten, 8:12, 13
   f. Fifth Trumpet—Fallen Star and Plague of Locusts, 9:1-12
   g. Sixth Trumpet—Angels Loosed at River Euphrates, 9:13-21
   h. Interlude Between the Sixth and Seventh Trumpets, 10:1-11:14
      (1). The Strong Angel with the Little Book, 10:1-7
      (2). John Eats the Little Book, 10:8-11
      (3). Date for the Ending of "The Times of the Gentiles," 11:1, 2
      (4). Duration of the Prophesying of the Two Witnesses, 11:3-12
      (5). Doom of the Second Woe—Great Earthquake, 11:13, 14
   i. Seventh Trumpet—End of Great Tribulation and Opening of Temple in Heaven, 11:15-19

3. **Seven Performers** During the Great Tribulation, chapters 12-13
   a. The Woman—Israel, 12:1, 2
   b. The Red Dragon—Satan, 12:3, 4
   c. The Child of the Woman—Jesus Christ, 12:5, 6
   d. Michael, the Archangel, Wars with the Dragon, 12:7-12
   e. The Dragon Persecutes the Woman, 12:13-16
   f. Remnant of Israel, 12:17
   g. Wild Beast Out of the Sea—a Political Power and a Person, 13:1-10
      (1). Wild Beast, Description, verses 1, 2
      (2). Wild Beast, Death Dealing Stroke, verse 3
      (3). Wild Beast, Deity Assumed, verses 4, 5
      (4). Wild Beast, Defying God, verses 6-8
      (5). Wild Beast, Defiance Denied to Anyone, verses 9, 10
   h. Wild Beast Out of the Earth—a Religious Leader, 13:11-18
      (1). Wild Beast, Description, verse 11
      (2). Wild Beast, Delegated Authority, verses 12-14
      (3). Wild Beast, Delusion Perpetrated on the World, verses 15-17
      (4). Wild Beast, Designation, verse 18

4. **Looking to the End of the Great Tribulation,** chapter 14
   a. Picture of the Lamb with the 144,00, verses 1-5
   b. Proclamation of the Everlasting Gospel, verses 6, 7
   c. Pronouncement of Judgment on Babylon, verse 8
   d. Pronouncement of Judgment on Those Who Received the Mark of the Beast, verses 9-12
   e. Praise for Those Who Die in the Lord, verse 13
   f. Preview of Armageddon, verses 14-20

5. Pouring Out of the **Seven Mixing Bowls of Wrath,** chapters 15, 16
   a. Preparation for Final Judgment of the Great Tribulation, 15:1-16:1
      (1). Tribulation Saints in Heaven Worship God Because He is Holy and Just, 15:1-4
      (2). Temple of the Tabernacle Opened in Heaven that Seven Angels, Having Seven Golden Bowls, Might Proceed Forth, 15:5-16:1
   b. Pouring Out of the First Bowl, 16:2
   c. Pouring Out of the Second Bowl, 16:3

d. Pouring Out of the Third Bowl, 16:4-7

e. Pouring Out of the Fourth Bowl, 16:8,9

f. Pouring Out of the Fifth Bowl, 16:10,11

g. Pouring Out of the Sixth Bowl, 16:12

h. Interlude: Kings of Inhabited Earth Proceed to Har-Magedon, 16:13-16

i. Pouring Out of the Seventh Bowl, 16:17-21

6. The **Two Babylons Judged,** chapters 17, 18

    a. The Apostate Church in the Great Tribulation, chapter 17

        (1). Great Harlot Riding the Wild Beast, verses 1-7

        (2). Wild Beast Destroys the Great Harlot, verses 8-18

    b. Political and Commercial Babylon Judged, chapter 18

        (1). Announcement of Fall of Commercial and Political Babylon, verses 1-8

        (2). Anguish in the World Because of Judgment on Babylon, verses 9-19

        (3). Anticipation of Joy in Heaven Because of Judgment on Babylon, verses 20-24

C. Marriage of the Lamb and Return of Christ in Judgment, chapter 19

    1. Four Hallelujahs, verses 1-6

    2. Bride of the Lamb and Marriage Supper, verses 7-10

    3. Return of Christ as King of Kings and Lord of Lords, verses 11-16

    4. Battle of Armageddon, verses 17,18

    5. Hell Opened, verses 19-21

D. Millennium, chapter 20

    1. Satan Bound 1000 Years, verses 1-3

    2. Saints of the Great Tribulation Reign with Christ 1000 Years, verses 4-6

    3. Satan Loosed After 1000 Years, verses 7-9

    4. Satan Cast Into Lake of Fire and Brimstone, verse 10

    5. Setting of Great White Throne Where Lost Are Judged and Follow Satan Into Lake of Fire and Brimstone, verses 11-15

E. Entrance Into Eternity; Eternity Unveiled, chapters 21,22

    1. New Heaven, New Earth, New Jerusalem, 21:1,2

    2. New Era, 21:3-8

    3. New Jerusalem, Description of the Eternal Abode of the Bride, 21:9-21

    4. New Relationship—God Dwelling with Man, 21:22,23

Chapter 1

THEME: The person of Jesus Christ—Christ in glory.

OUTLINE:

I. The PERSON of Jesus Christ—Christ in Glory, chapter 1

A. Title of the Book, verse 1

B. Method of Revelation, verse 2

C. Beatitude of Bible Study, verse 3

D. Greetings from John the Writer, and from Jesus Christ in Heaven, verses 4-8

E. The Post-Incarnate Christ in a Glorified Body, Judging His Church (the Great High Priest in the Holy of Holies), verses 9-18
"we know him no longer after the flesh"

F. Time Division of the Contents of the Apocalypse, verse 19

G. Interpretation of the Seven Stars and Seven Lampstands, verse 20

REMARKS:

The major theme of the entire Bible is the Lord Jesus Christ. The Scriptures are both theocentric and Christocentric. Since Christ is God, He is the One who fills the horizon of the Word of God. This needs to be kept in mind in the book of Revelation more than in any book of the Bible, even more than in the Gospels. The Bible tells what He has done, is doing, and will do. Revelation emphasizes what He is going to do.

COMMENT:

A. Title of the Book, verse 1

Verse 1—The Revelation of Jesus Christ, which God gave unto him, to show unto his servants things which must shortly come to pass; and he sent and signified it by his angel unto his servant John:

The unveiling of Jesus Christ which God gave Him to show unto His bond servants things which must shortly come to pass completely, and He sent and signified (gave a sign) it by His angel (messenger) to His servant John.

The word *revelation* is in the Greek *apocalypse* and means *unveiling*. This word occurs 18 times in the New Testament—

1 time in the Gospels (Luke 2:32)
13 times in Paul's Epistles (Gal. 1:12; II Thes. 1:7)
3 times in Peter's Epistles (I Pet.. 1:7)

To show means word pictures, symbols, direct and indirect representations.

Signified—symbols are symbolic of reality (II Peter 1:20). Ottman said, "The figurative language of Revelation is figurative of facts."

Things assure us that they are not ethereal and ephemeral dream-stuff. There is a hard core of real facts in this book.

Must—urgent necessity and absolute certainty.

Shortly, as God records time (II Pet. 3:9). See Luke 18:8 where delay is implied, also where imminence is implied. Compare Romans 16:20 and Revelation 22:6. Events in this book refer to the future.

Come to pass has a note of finality—not begin to come to pass but come to pass in entirety.

THE STEPS OF REVELATION

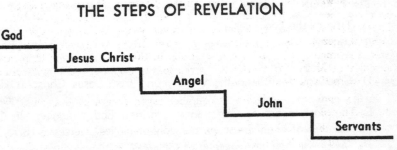

B. Method of Revelation, verse 2

Verse 2—Who bare record of the word of God, and of the testimony of Jesus Christ, and of all things that he saw.

Who bore witness of the Word of God, and of the testimony (witness of) Jesus Christ even as many things as he saw.

Bore witness is in the Greek an epistolary aorist. John places himself with the readers who consider the writing as taking place in the past.

Word of God refers both to Christ and to the contents of this book.

Testimony is *witness*. This word occurs 90 times in the writings of John (50 times in his Gospel).

He saw—John was an eye witness of the visions.

C. Beatitude of Bible Study, verse 3

Verse 3—Blessed is he that readeth, and they that hear the words of this prophecy, and keep those things which are written therein: for the time is at hand.

Blessed—this book opens with a beatitude and not with a curse. (Other beatitudes in this book are in 14:13; 16:15; 19:9; 20:6; 22:7; 22:14.) There are seven beatitudes in this book.

He that readeth—the reader in the church, the teacher.
They that hear—the churches, the believers in the class.
And keep—the teacher and the church, all believers.
At hand means near.

D. Greetings from John the Writer, and from Jesus Christ in Heaven, verses 4-8

Verse 4—John to the seven churches which are in Asia: Grace be unto you, and peace, from him which is, and which was, and which is to come; and from the seven Spirits which are before his throne;

12

John—note the absence of all titles. John was recognized as to his place and position. There are no titles in heaven.

Seven—numbers carried a religious meaning to the people of John's day that is foreign to us today. The number seven was a sacred number which denoted completeness, but more particularly it had to do with God's covenant dealings with Israel: the sabbath (7th day), Ex. 31:13-17; circumcision, Gen. 17:12; worship, Lev. 4:6, 17.

Jericho was encompassed seven times; Naaman dipped seven times in Jordan, etc. See also Deut. 28:7, 25; I Sam. 2:5; Lev. 26:21, 24; Psa. 79:12. There were seven years of plenty and seven years of famine in Joseph's time. Nebuchadnezzar was insane for seven years. There are seven beatitudes in the New Testament; there are seven petitions in the Lord's prayer; there are seven parables in Matt. 13; there were seven loaves which fed the multitude; Jesus spoke seven times from the cross, etc.

In the book of Revelation the number seven occurs so frequently that even the casual reader must notice it.

Actually there were more than seven churches in Asia (e.g. churches at Colossae, Miletus, Hieropolis), but seven are representative of the whole church.

Asia refers to the proconsular province which included Lydia, Mysia, Caria and parts of Phrygia. It does not mean the continent of Asia or Asia Minor. Asia Minor is a term not used until the 4th century A.D.

Grace is *charis*, the Greek form of greeting.

Peace is *shalom*, the Hebrew form of greeting. Peace flows from grace, which is the source of all blessings.

From him—the greeting is trinitarian. God the Father is referred to here.

Which is, and which was, and which is to come emphasizes the eternity and immutability of God.

Seven Spirits refer to the Holy Spirit (seven branches of the lampstand).

Verse 5—And from Jesus Christ, who is the faithful witness, and the first begotten of the dead, and the prince of the kings of the earth, Unto him that loved us, and washed us from our sins in his own blood,

Jesus Christ refers to God the Son. The desire and work of the Trinity is to glorify the Son (John 17:5).

Titles, the sevenfold identification of Jesus Christ:

(1) *Faithful witness*—Jesus Christ is the trustworthy witness to the facts of this book. The facts are about Him. He testifies of Himself.

(2) *The first born of the dead*—*first born* is from the Greek word *prototokos*. He is the first to rise from the dead, never to die again. Death was a womb which bore Him. His own will follow Him in resurrection (I Thes. 4:14).

(3) *The ruler of the kings of the earth* speaks of His ultimate position during the Millennium (Phil. 2:9-11).

(4) *Unto Him that loves* is in the present tense and emphasizes His constant attitude toward His own.

(5) *Loosed us from our sins in His own blood* (see I Tim. 2:5 and I Pet. 1:18).

13

Verse 6—And hath made us kings and priests unto God and his Father; to him be glory and dominion for ever and ever. Amen.

(6) *And hath made us a kingdom of priests unto His God and Father*—believers are never called kings. They are to rule with Him.

His Father in a sense that He is not our Father. It is the relationship in the Trinity.

(7) *To Him the glory* (praise) *and the dominion unto the ages of the ages* [eternity emphasized]. *Amen.* Jesus Christ is both the subject and the object of this book. He is the mover of all events and all events move toward Him. He is the far off eternal purpose in everything. All things were made for Him.

Verse 7—Behold, he cometh with clouds; and every eye shall see him, and they also which pierced him: and all kindreds of the earth shall wail because of him. Even so, Amen.

Behold, He cometh with clouds denotes the personal and physical coming of Christ (see Acts 1:10, 11; Matt. 24:27-30; Mark 14:62).

Every eye shall see Him—it will be a physical and bodily appearance, an appeal to the eye-gate.

They also which pierced Him (see John 19:34) includes all those who have turned their backs upon Him.

All the tribes of the earth shall beat their breasts because of Him. This will be the reaction of all Christ rejecters.

Even so, Amen means *Yea, faithful.*

Verse 8—I am Alpha and Omega, the beginning and the ending, saith the Lord, which is, and which was, and which is to come, the Almighty.

I am the Alpha and Omega. The alpha and omega are the first and last letters of the Greek alphabet. He is the Word of God—the full revelation and intelligent communication of God. Here the emphasis is upon the beginning and the ending. The Omega is not spelled out as is the Alpha. The ending is not yet complete. He will complete God's program.

The beginning and the ending refers to the eternity of the Son and His immutability (see Heb. 13:8).

Saith the Lord the God is an affirmation of the deity of Christ.

Which is—at the present time, the glorified Christ.

Which was—past time, the first coming of Christ as Saviour.

Which is to come—future time, the second coming of Christ as Sovereign.

E. The Post-Incarnate Christ in a Glorified Body, Judging His Church (the Great High Priest in the Holy of Holies), verses 9-18

Verse 9—I John, who also am your brother, and companion in tribulation, and in the kingdom and patience of Jesus Christ, was in the isle that is called Patmos, for the word of God, and for the testimony of Jesus Christ.

I, John, who am your brother, and partaker with you in the persecution (for Christ's sake), and kingdom and patience in Jesus; I was (found myself) in the isle called Patmos because of (on account of—"dia") the Word of God and the witness of Jesus. (See Dan. 10:2.)

John is not referring to the Great Tribulation, but to the persecution that was already befalling the believers (II Tim. 3:12).

Kingdom refers to the present state of the kingdom (John 3:3). By virtue of the new birth which places a sinner in Christ, he is likewise in the kingdom (Col. 1:16 ASV). This is not the Millennial Kingdom which Christ institutes at His coming. Someone has said, "It is now the kingdom and patience."

John explains the reason he was on the isle of Patmos. He was exiled there from about 86 to 96 A.D. It is a rugged, volcanic island off the coast of Asia Minor. It is about 10 miles long and 6 miles wide.

Jesus is the name used by John in his gospel and apocalypse.

Verses 10, 11—I was in the Spirit on the Lord's day, and heard behind me a great voice, as of a trumpet, saying, I am Alpha and Omega, the first and the last: and, What thou seest, write in a book, and send it unto the seven churches, which are in Asia; unto Ephesus, and unto Smyrna, and unto Pergamos, and unto Thyatira, and unto Sardis, and unto Philadelphia, and unto Laodicea.

I was (found myself) in (the) Spirit in the Lord's Day, and heard behind me a great sound, as of a (war) trumpet, saying, What you are seeing, write (promptly) into a book, and send (promptly) to the seven churches, unto Ephesus, and unto Smyrna, and unto Pergamos, and unto Thyatira, and unto Sardis, and unto Philadelphia, and unto Laodicea.

The Holy Spirit is here performing His office work (John 16:13, 14).

John is here giving a panoramic view like a motion picture—and this is really cinerama. It is sight and sound—an appeal to both the eye gate and the ear gate. These seven churches were located in the province of Asia whose mountains were in view of the isle of Patmos.

Verses 12, 13—And I turned to see the voice that spake with me. And being turned, I saw seven golden candlesticks; and in the midst of the seven candlesticks one like unto the Son of man, clothed with a garment down to the foot, and girt about the paps with a golden girdle.

And I turned to see the voice which was speaking with me, and when I turned, I saw seven golden lampstands, and in the midst of the lampstands One like to a Son of Man, clothed with a garment, reaching to the foot, and girt about the breasts with a golden girdle

The seven golden lampstands remind us of the Tabernacle. There it was one lampstand with seven branches. Here it is seven separate lampstands. Since these lampstands represent seven separate churches (verse 20), the difference is explained. The function of all is the same—"Ye are the light of the world."

Christ's work on earth in the past for redemption centered about the brazen altar in the outer court. The brazen altar speaks of the cross of Christ.

The golden lampstands speak of Christ's present work in heaven in maintaining the lights. Aaron lighted the lamps in the Tabernacle, put them out with snuffers, filled them with oil and trimmed the wicks (Ex. 3:7, 8; 37:23; 40:25), such is the work of Christ with His own.

A Son of Man is identified as the Lord Jesus (compare John 5:25 with John 5:27; Rev. 14:14).

The garments are those of the High Priest (Ex. 28:2-4). *Coat* (Ex. 28:39) represents the inherent righteousness of Christ. "In Him . . . is no sin." "He . . . who knew no sin."

Girdle. Josephus states that the priests were girded about the breasts. The ordinary custom was to be girded about the loins. But the emphasis here is not on service but on strength. It speaks of His judgment in truth (Isa. 22:21; Eph. 6:14).

We are asked to consider our Great High Priest as He stands in the midst of the churches judging believers—that the lights might continue to shine (I Cor. 11:31, 32). He sometimes uses the snuffers (I John 5:16). This definitely is not a picture of Christ in His work of intercession before the golden altar of incense; He is judging, not interceding. Only the lampstands are called to our attention here.

Verses 14, 15—His head and his hairs were white like wool, as white as snow; and his eyes were as a flame of fire; and his feet like unto fine brass, as if they burned in a furnace; and his voice as the sound of many waters.

His hair . . . as white as snow speaks of His eternity, "Ancient of days" (Dan. 7:9) and his dignity.

His eyes as a flame of fire speaks of His penetrating insight and eye-witness of the total life of the Church. He sat over the treasury and watched how the people gave; His eyes met those of Simon Peter after he had denied Him.

His feet like unto burnished brass continues the thought of judgment. The brazen altar is where sin was judged.

His voice as the sound of many waters is the voice of authority—the voice that called this universe into existence, the voice that will raise His own from the grave. (Compare Ezek. 1:24 and Psalm 29).

All these figures add to the picture of Christ as High Priest, inspecting and judging His Church.

Verse 16—And he had in his right hand seven stars: and out of his mouth went a sharp twoedged sword: and his countenance was as the sun shineth in his strength.

Seven stars are identified in verse 20.

Out of his mouth . . . a sword, two-edged, sharp represents His Word (Heb. 4:12). God judges by His Word—He does so today. How do you measure up to His Word?

His appearance . . . as the sun shineth in his strength reveals the impression made upon John. He could not look steadily upon Him any more than we can look upon the sun.

John does not record the Transfiguration in his gospel, he records it here. This vision is not grotesque but is a solemn representation of Christ after His ascension. Granted that figures are used, they set before us facts. They are representations of reality.

Verses 17, 18—And when I saw him, I fell at his feet as dead. And he laid his right hand upon me, saying unto me, Fear not; I am the first and the last: I am he that liveth, and was dead; and, behold, I am alive for evermore, Amen; and have the keys of hell and of death.

16

The effect of the vision upon John was nothing short of paralyzing. This is the man who reclined upon the bosom of Jesus in the upper room.

Fear not is the greeting of Deity addressing humanity. There are given four reasons for not fearing:

(1) *I am the first and the last* speaks of His deity. He is first because there were none before Him and He is last for there are none to follow.

(2) *And the living one who became dead* speaks of His redemptive death and resurrection.

(3) *And, behold I am alive for evermore* speaks of His present state and session.

(4) *And have the keys of death and of hades* (the unseen world). The keys speak of authority and power (Matt. 16:19). Jesus has power over death and the grave now because of His own death and resurrection (John 5:21-29; 11:25, 26). *Hades* is the Greek word for the unseen world. It can refer to the grave where the body is laid or to the place where the spirit goes.

F. Time Division of the Contents of the Apocalypse, verse 19

Verse 19—Write the things which thou hast seen, and the things which are, and the things which shall be hereafter;

Write therefore the things which you have seen, and the things which are, and the things which you are about to see after these things (meta tauta).

This gives the chronological division of the book into three time periods of past, present, and future. Verse 18 gives the division according to the person and work of Christ. The apocalypse tells what Jesus has done, is doing, and is going to do. Keep your eye on Him and not on the things— churches, seals, beasts, and bowls—which are secondary. He is the Person to behold. This is the revelation of Jesus Christ. This book is Christocentric.

G. Interpretation of the Seven Stars and Seven Lampstands, verse 20

Verse 20—The mystery of the seven stars which thou sawest in my right hand, and the seven golden candlesticks. The seven stars are the angels of the seven churches: and the seven candlesticks which thou sawest are the seven churches.

Mystery means sacred secret, that which has not been revealed until the time of this writing. It pertains here specifically to that which John has seen.

Seven stars are identified as the *seven angels*.

Stars represent authority (Num. 24:17; Dan. 12:3). Apostates are called wandering stars (Jude 13).

Angels can be either human or divine—the word is messenger. It could refer to a member of the angelic host of heaven; it could refer to a ruler or teacher of the congregation. (Personally, I like to think that it refers to the local pastors. It is good to hear a pastor being called an angel—sometimes we are called other things).

Seven golden lampstands represent the seven churches of Asia (see verse 11).

Chapters 2, 3

INTRODUCTION

OUTLINE:

II. The POSSESSION of Jesus Christ—The Church in the World, chaps. 2, 3

A. Letter of Christ to the Church in Ephesus, 2:1-7

B. Letter of Christ to the Church in Smyrna, 2:8-11

C. Letter of Christ to the Church in Pergamum, 2:12-17

D. Letter of Christ to the Church in Thyatira, 2:18-29

E. Letter of Christ to the Church in Sardis, 3:1-6

F. Letter of Christ to the Church in Philadelphia, 3:7-13

G. Letter of Christ to the Church in Laodicea, 3:14-22

These two chapters give the messages of Christ to the 7 churches. After chapter 3 the church is conspicuous by its absence. Up to chapter 4 the church is mentioned 19 times. From chapter 4 through chapter 20 (the Great White Throne Judgment) the church is not mentioned one time. The normal reaction is to inquire as to the destination and location of the church during this period. It is not in the world.

These 7 letters have a threefold interpretation and application:

(1) Contemporary—they had a direct message to the local churches of John's day.

(2) Composite—there is something that is applicable to all churches in all ages in each message to each individual church.

(3) Chronological—the panoramic history of the church is given in these 7 letters from Pentecost to the Parousia, from the upper room to the upper air. There are 7 distinct periods of church history. Ephesus represents the apostolic church: Laodicea represents the apostate church. This prophetic picture is largely fulfilled and is now church history.

The Lord follows a well defined and definite format in addressing each church:

(1) Some feature of the glorified Christ from the vision in chapter one is emphasized in addressing each church.

(2) The letters are addressed to the angel of each church.

(3) He begins by stating to each, "I know thy works."

(4) He first gives a commendation, then a condemnation. The exceptions should be noted: there is no word of condemnation to Smyrna or Philadelphia; there is no word of commendation to Laodicea.

(5) Each letter concludes with the warning, "He that hath an ear, let him hear what the Spirit saith. . . ."

Chapter 2

A. The Letter of Christ to the Church in Ephesus—The Apostolic Church—
Pentecost to 100 A.D., **2:1-7.**

Ephesus was the chief city of the province of Asia. It was called "the Vanity
Fair of Asia." Pliny called it "the Light of Asia." It was both the religious
and commercial center of that entire area which influenced both east and west
—Europe and Asia. The temple of Diana was there which was one of the seven
wonders of the ancient world, being the largest Greek temple ever constructed
(418 feet, 1 inch by 239 feet, 4½ inches). There were over 100 external
columns about 56 feet in height of which 36 were hand carved. It was built
over a marsh on an artificial foundation of skins and charcoal so that it was
not affected by earthquakes. The doors were of cypress wood; columns and
walls were of Parian marble; the staircase was carved out of one vine from
Cyprus.

The temple served as the bank of Asia and was the depository of vast sums
of money. It was an art gallery displaying the masterpieces of Praxiteles,
Phidias, Scopas, and Polycletus. Apelles' famous painting of Alexander was
there. Behind a purple curtain was the lewd and crude image of Diana, the
goddess of fertility. She was many breasted, carried a club in one hand and
a trident in the other. "Horrible is Diana of the Ephesians" could be accurately
substituted for "Great is Diana of the Ephesians."

Paul met great opposition in Ephesus but he did his greatest work here (Acts
19). See especially Acts 19:10 and I Corinthians 16:8, 9.

**Verse 1—Unto the angel of the church of Ephesus write; These things saith
he that holdeth the seven stars in his right hand, who walketh in the midst
of the seven golden candlesticks;**

*Unto the messenger of the church in Ephesus write; These things saith the
One holding the seven stars in His right hand, the One walking (up and down)
in the midst of the seven golden lampstands.*

Messenger is a more normal translation than *angel*. Since it would seem
rather futile to address these letters to angelic creatures in heaven, evidently
the teacher or leader of the church is intended.

In Ephesus is accurate. The church is *in* the world but not *of* the world.

Christ is seen here in complete control of the messengers of the church. He
is not standing but walking up and down which denotes freedom, activity, and
full inspection of the churches. Christ is so engaged today.

**Verses 2, 3—I know thy works, and thy labour, and thy patience, and how
thou canst not bear them which are evil: and thou hast tried them which say
they are apostles, and are not, and hast found them liars: and hast borne,
and hast patience, and for my name's sake hast laboured, and hast not
fainted.**

There are seven words of commendation.

(1) *Works* means good works (Ephesians 2:8-10; Titus 1:16; 3:5, 8; Hebrews 9:14).

19

(2) *Labor* speaks of the person and not his works. There is a note of weariness in the word—"Jesus being wearied with his journey. . . ." There is also the note of suffering although this is not the martyr church (II Timothy 3:12).

(3) *Patience* is the fruit of the Holy Spirit (II Peter 1:5-6; James 1:2-4).

(4) *Not bear . . . evil men*—the church was patient but not with evil men. The early church had spiritual discernment (see Ananias and Sapphira, Acts 5:1-11). We are not to tolerate trouble makers (Romans 16:17; II Thessalonians 3:6; II John).

(5) *Didst try . . . apostles.* The church in Ephesus loved the apostles. Paul had founded this church (Acts 20:29, 31) and John had been their pastor. One was not an apostle unless he had seen the resurrected Christ. These Christians tested a man for his doctrine (Acts 2:42).

(6) *Hast borne . . . for my name's sake*—they preached Christ.

(7) *Hast not grown weary*—the church had spiritual stamina and strength. It was virile, vital, and vigorous.

Verse 4—Nevertheless I have somewhat against thee, because thou hast left thy first love.

Nevertheless I have against thee that thou didst leave thy best (first) love.

This is the one word of condemnation. They had lost that intense and enthusiastic devotion to the person of Christ. It is difficult for us to sense the state to which the Holy Spirit had brought this church.

Verse 5—Remember therefore from whence thou art fallen, and repent, and do the first works; or else I will come unto thee quickly, and will remove thy candlestick out of his place, except thou repent.

They were called to do three things for restoration: (1) remember, (2) repent, (3) return.

I will remove thy lampstand is the warning. Their testimony would be taken from them. The church in Ephesus has been gone for centuries—smothered by the Moslems. There is not a Christian church within miles of Ephesus.

Verse 6—But this thou hast, that thou hatest the deeds of the Nicolaitans, which I also hate.

Nicolaitans is a compound word. *Nikao* means to conquer and *laos* means the people. Although it is difficult to identify this cult, there are three (3) possible explanations:

(1) From the meaning of the name, "rulers of the people" (laity), we know that there was appearing a distinction between clergy and laity. That a priestly order was beginning to take shape is the common explanation.

(2) There is no way of identifying this group with any in early or late church history.

(3) Nicolaus of Antioch, who apostatized from the truth, formed an Antinomian Gnostic cult which taught that one must indulge in sin in order to understand it. They gave themselves over to sensuality with the explanation that such sins did not touch the spirit. That Nicolaitans refers to this cult is the most

likely explanation. The Ephesus church hated it, but the church in Pergamos tolerated it.

Verse 7—He that hath an ear, let him hear what the Spirit saith unto the churches; To him that overcometh will I give to eat of the tree of life, which is in the midst of the paradise of God.

He that hath an ear—This is a phrase used by Christ to alert dull ears (Matthew 11:15). He speaks to those with spiritual perception.

The Spirit is the Holy Spirit. He is the teacher of the church (I Corinthians 2:14).

To him that overcometh refers to the genuine believer (Romans 8:37; II Corinthians 2:14; I John 5:4).

Will I give to eat of the tree of life—Man was forbidden to eat of this tree after the fall (Genesis 3:22-24). In heaven the "no trespassing" sign will be down and they will be given the privilege of eating of the tree of life.

Paradise of God means the *garden of God* (Revelation 22:1-6). Heaven is a garden of green primarily and not just a place with streets of gold.

B. The Letter of Christ to the Church in Smyrna (Myrrh, Exodus 30:23; Song of Solomon 3:6)—The Martyr Church 100 A.D. to approximately 314 A.D., **2:8-11.**

Smyrna, called "the glory of Asia," was north of Ephesus, on the Smyrna gulf. Destroyed in 627 B.C. by the Lydians, it remained a ghost town for 400 years. The rebuilding of this city was planned by Alexander and completed after his death. Considered the most brilliant city of Asia Minor, it was celebrated for its schools of science and medicine, for its handsome buildings and wide, paved streets. The temple of Cybele and Dionysius (Bacchus, the god of wine) was there. To this city Christ addressed His briefest message— and it was all commendatory.

Verse 8—And unto the angel of the church in Symrna write; These things saith the first and the last, which was dead, and is alive;

And to the messenger of the church in Smyrna, write, These things saith the first and the last, who became dead, and lived. (See 1:17-18).

The Lord chose from the vision of Himself that particular figure which was fitting for each church.

The first and the last means that there was nothing before Him and nothing is to follow. The final disposition of all things is in Him. The persecuted believers needed to know this. "From the vanishing point to the vanishing point thou art God" (Psalm 90:2).

Who became dead, and lived speaks of the death and resurrection of Christ. His experience with death identified Him with the 5 millions who were martyred during this period. He was triumphant over death and can save to the uttermost those who are enduring persecution and martyrdom.

Verses 9, 10—I know thy works, and tribulation, and poverty, (but thou art rich) and I know the blasphemy of them which say they are Jews, and are not, but are the synagogue of Satan. Fear none of those things which thou shalt suffer: behold, the devil shall cast some of you into prison, that ye may

21

be tried; and ye shall have tribulation ten days: be thou faithful unto death, and I will give thee a crown of life.

There are seven (7) things in this church which the Lord commended:

(1) *Tribulation* is mentioned first. *Works* are not in the best manuscripts. This is not the great tribulation. Since the awful persecution of the church by the Roman Emperors is not called the Great Tribulation, surely our small sufferings are not the Great Tribulation.

(2) *Poverty* denotes the lack of material possessions. The early church was made up largely of the poorer classes. When the wealthy believed, their property was confiscated because of their faith. *But thou art rich* denotes the spiritual wealth of the church (Ephesus 2:7; Hebrews 11:26). Note the contrast to the church of Laodicea (Revelation 3:17, 18).

(3) These were Jews outwardly. There only has been a remnant of these people who truly have been God's people (Romans 11:5). It is his religion that makes a man a Jew. Smyrna was a city of culture in which many Jews had discarded their belief in the Old Testament.

(4) *Fear nothing* is the encouragement of the Lord to His own in the midst of persecutions. This is the second time in this book that the Lord has offered this encouragement (1:17). History tells us that multitudes went to their death singing praises to God.

(5) The devil and *Satan* are the same person. We shall consider this fearful creature later. Christ labels him as being responsible for the suffering of the saints. We tend to blame the immediate person or circumstance which serves as Satan's tool.

(6) *Tribulation ten days.* There were 10 intense periods of persecution by 10 Roman Emperors:

Nero—A.D. 64-68 (Paul beheaded)

Domitian—95-96 (John exiled)

Trajan—104-117 (Ignatius burned at the stake)

Marcus Aurelius—161-180 (Polycarp martyred)

Severus—200-211

Maximinius—235-237

Decius—250-253

Valerian—257-260

Aurelian—270-275

Diocletian—303-313 (the worst emperor)

(7) *Faithful unto death* means martyrdom.

Crown of life—This is a special crown for those who suffer (James 1:12). The Lord will reward believers for their lives down here.

Verse 11—He that hath an ear, let him hear what the Spirit saith unto the churches; He that overcometh shall not be hurt of the second death.

Second death (Revelation 20:6, 14; 21:8). No believer will experience the second death. The first death concerns the body: the second death the soul and spirit (I John 5:4; John 5:24).

C. The Letter of Christ to the Church in Pergamum—Paganism Unlimited (the world begins to enter the church)—314 A.D. to approximately 590 A.D., 2:12-17.

Pergamum was a city in Mysia, labeled by Pliny "by far the most illustrious of Asia." Its beautiful buildings distinguished it as the most beautiful city in the East. Art and literature were encouraged and it boasted a library of 200,000 volumes. Later the library was given by Antony to Cleopatra and subsequently became the famed library at Alexandria. The volumes were of parchment which was first used here. Pergamum was the religious center of the province. Here was the temple of Esculapius, the god of healing, represented by a living serpent—a return to the worship of Satan.

Verse 12—And to the angel of the church in Pergamos write; These things saith he which hath the sharp sword with two edges;

Sharp sword with two edges (1:16). Christ corrects the church with His Word (John 17:17; Hebrews 4:12; I Corinthians 11:31-32). The Word is not only a way through the world, but a way to keep the world out of the church. The sword is for judging believers.

Verse 13—I know thy works, and where thou dwellest, even where Satan's seat is: and thou holdest fast my name, and hast not denied my faith, even in those days wherein Antipas was my faithful martyr, who was slain among you, where Satan dwelleth.

There are three things which the Lord commends in this church.

(1) *Where thou dwellest.* The Lord takes note of the circumstances of believers.

Even where Satan's throne is reveals that religion is big business with Satan as there were so many pagan temples in Pergamum. Satan is not in hell (Revelation 20:1-3), but is prince of this world, controlling kingdoms, and going up and down the earth as a roaring lion seeking whom he may devour.

(2) *Holdest fast my name* reveals that even when the world was coming in, the Church stood for the name of Christ. This period produced giants of the faith. Athanasius, from North Africa, forever answered the Arian heresy as to the person of Christ. The Council at Nicaea condemned Arianism, 325 A.D., which contended that Christ was a created being. Augustine answered Pelagianism which denied original sin, total corruption of the human nature, and irresistible grace.

(3) *And hast not denied my faith* means the body of true doctrine which is believed by Christians.

Antipas is the name of one of the many unknown martyrs of this period—known only to the Lord.

Verse 14—But I have a few things against thee, because thou hast there them that hold the doctrine of Balaam, who taught Balac to cast a stumblingblock before the children of Israel, to eat things sacrificed unto idols, and to commit fornication.

There are two items for condemnation: (1) the doctrine of Balaam and (2) the doctrine of the Nicolaitans.

23

(1) *Doctrine of Balaam* (see Numbers 25:1-9, note that the "error of Balaam", Jude 11, was that he thought a holy God would curse Israel; and the "way of Balaam", II Peter 2:15, was covetousness). When Balaam could not curse Israel he told Balak that by sending the Moabite women into the camp of Israel he would bring about fornication and the introduction of idolatry into the homes through mixed marriages. From Genesis to Revelation God warns against intermarriage of believer and unbeliever.

It was in this period of church history that the world entered the church, spiritual worship was destroyed and pagan practices (images and the virgin and child) were introduced. When the devil found that he could not hurt the church from the outside, he joined the church and did his work on the inside.

Verse 15—So hast thou also them that hold the doctrine of the Nicolaitans, which thing I hate.

(2) *Doctrine of the Nicolaitans.* The church in Ephesus hated this (verse 6) but the church in Pergamum tolerated it. It was *deeds* in Ephesus; it is *doctrine* here. The doctrine of Balaam, which permits heathen religious rituals, leads to the doctrine of the Nicolaitans which sanctions immoral practices.

Which thing I hate. Christ hates as well as loves.

Verse 16—Repent; or else I will come unto thee quickly, and will fight against them with the sword of my mouth.

The only cure is repentance (*metanoeson*, a change of mind), I John 1:9. *Sword of my mouth.* The only answer is the Word of God.

Verse 17—He that hath an ear, let him hear what the Spirit saith unto the churches; To him that overcometh will I give to eat of the hidden manna, and will give him a white stone, and in the stone a new name written, which no man knoweth saving he that receiveth it.

To him that overcometh is the definition of a genuine Christian (I John 5:4, 5; Romans 8:37-39). The believer knows that the victory is won by Christ and not by himself (Phil. 1:6).

Hidden manna suggests the manna in the wilderness and the pot of manna placed in the Ark (Heb. 9:4). It speaks of the person and death of Christ (John 6:32-35). The believer needs to feed on Christ. This is a must for spiritual growth. Christ is hidden from view today.

White stone suggests that the believer is not blackballed. This is a difficult figure to interpret. "White is everywhere the color and livery of heaven," says Trench. The stone may suggest the Urim of the High Priest. Dean Plumptre suggests that this is a reference to the custom of sending a token to a friend with his name upon it as an admission to a feast or event.

New name evidently refers to a new name of Christ and not a new name for the believer. The believer will continue to learn more about Christ throughout eternity. He will mean something personal to each believer that He means to no one else.

D. The Letter of Christ to the Church in Thyatira—The Pagan Church (rise of Romanism, the Dark Ages)—590 to approximately 1517 A.D., **2:18-29**

Thyatira was situated "on the confines of Mysia and Ionia," according to Vincent. It was first a Macedonian colony established by Alexander. It became

24

prosperous under the sponsorship of Vespasian, the Roman Emperor. Thyatira was headquarters for many ancient guilds, as the potters, tanners, weavers, robe makers and dyers guilds. It was the center of the dyeing industry. Lydia, the seller of purple, who in Philippi became Paul's first convert in Europe, came from here (Acts 16:14). Apollos, the sun god, was worshipped here as Tyrimnos.

Verse 18—And unto the angel of the church in Thyatira write; These things saith the Son of God, who hath his eyes like unto a flame of fire, and his feet are like fine brass;

Son of God, a substitute for *son of man* (Revelation 1:13), occurs only once in this book. Evidently these two titles are synonymous.

Eyes as a flame of fire, referring to Revelation 1:14, reveals that He is searching out this church in a particular manner.

Feet like burnished brass, from the vision in Revelation 1:15, reveals that He is judging this church—though His patience is also manifest (verse 21). False religion in the form of heathen practices enter the church in this period.

Verse 19—I know thy works, and charity, and service, and faith, and thy patience, and thy works; and the last to be more than the first.

I know thy works, and love, and faith, and ministry, and patience, and that thy last works are more than the first.

Here are six words of commendation to the Church in the Dark Ages where there were many true believers who had a personal love of Christ which was manifested in works.

(1) *Works* were the credentials of true believers. There were many who lived spotless lives and by their good works "adorned the doctrine."

(2) *Love.* Although love was growing cold in the Ephesian period, it had not completely died out even in the Dark Ages. Bernard of Clairvaux, Peter Waldo, John Wycliffe, John Huss, Savonarola, and Anselm were among a great company of believers who, during this period, maintained good works, a love for the truth, and an allegiance to the faith.

(3) *Faith,* though it is placed after works and love in this instance, is the mainspring that turns the hands of works and love.

(4) *Ministry* is service.

(5) *Patience* is endurance in days of darkness.

(6) *Thy last works are more than the first.* In this church, works increased rather than diminished.

All six virtues are produced within the believers by the Holy Spirit.

There is one (1) frightful charge of condemnation:

Verse 20—Notwithstanding I have a few things against thee, because thou sufferest that woman Jezebel, which calleth herself a prophetess, to teach and to seduce my servants to commit fornication, and to eat things sacrificed unto idols.

But I have against you that you tolerate the woman (wife) Jezebel, who calls herself the prophetess, and she teaches and seduces my servants to commit fornication and to eat things sacrificed to idols.

25

Evidently there was in the local church at Thyatira, a woman who had a reputation as a teacher and prophetess, who was the counterpart of Jezebel, the consort of Ahab (I Kings 16:29-19:21; 21:1-29; II Kings 9:22-37; Jeremiah 4:30; Nahum 3:4).

During this period idolatry and pagan practices mingled with Christian worship. The papacy was elevated to a place of secular power under Gregory I (590 A.D.), and later by Gregory VII, better known as Hildebrand, (1073-1085 A.D.). The introduction of rituals and church doctrine supplanted personal faith in Jesus Christ. Worship of the virgin and child and the mass were made a definite part of the church service. Purgatory became a positive doctrine and mass was said for the dead. The spurious documents labeled Donation of Constantine and Decretals of Isidore were circulated to give power and rulership to the pope.

As Jezebel killed Naboth and persecuted God's prophets, so the Roman Church instituted the Inquisition during this period.

Seduce means a "fundamental departure from the truth" (Vincent).

Jezebel stands in sharp contrast to Lydia, who came from Thyatira (Acts 16:14). Jezebel is merely a forerunner of the apostate church (Revelation 17:1-18).

Verse 21—And I gave her space to repent of her fornication; and she repented not.

Space is time. The Lord Jesus Christ has patiently dealt with this false system for over a thousand years. Rome boasts that she never changes—*semper idem*, always the same.

Verse 22—Behold, I will cast her into a bed, and them that commit adultery with her into great tribulation, except they repent of their deeds.

This is not a bed of pleasure but of punishment. The profession of Christianity while practicing heathen rites is spiritual adultery.

Great tribulation could refer to the persecution that Rome is enduring under Communism, or it may mean the Great Tribulation into which the apostate church will go (Revelation 17:1-18).

Their deeds should be translated *her* deeds.

Verse 23—And I will kill her children with death; and all the churches shall know that I am he which searcheth the reins and hearts: and I will give unto every one of you according to your works.

Children are those who were brought up under this system.

Let them be put to death with death (Vincent) refers to the second death.

All the churches—the Church of all the ages.

Reins means literally *kidneys* and refers to the total psychological make-up —thoughts, feelings and purposes.

According to your works speaks of judgment.

Verse 24—But unto you I say, and unto the rest in Thyatira, as many as have not this doctrine, and which have not known the depths of Satan, as they speak; I will put upon you none other burden.

26

But I say to you, to the rest in Thyatira, who do not hold this doctrine, which are of those who have not known the depths of Satan, as they say, I will put upon you none other burden (weight)."

This evidently had a local meaning for the Thyatira church which is not fully understood by us.

The depths of Satan refers perhaps to a gnostic sect know as the *Ophites*, who worshipped a serpent. They made a parody of Paul's words (I Corinthians 2:10). All heresy boasts of superior spiritual perception. The application to us, as twentieth century believers, is to refrain from heretical systems which destroy the simplicity of obedience to the Gospel.

Verse 25—But that which ye have already hold fast till I come.

Hold fast to the Word of God for we do not know when the Lord will come.

Till I come is a conditional clause which denotes the uncertainty of the hour in which He will come.

Verse 26—And he that overcometh, and keepeth my works unto the end, to him will I give power over the nations:

The works of Christ are in contrast to the works of Jezebel. The works of Christ are wrought by the Holy Spirit. We overcome by faith and not by effort.

Give power (authority) *over the nations* is explained by I Corinthians 6:2.

Verse 27—And he shall rule them with a rod of iron; as the vessels of a potter shall they be broken to shivers: even as I received of my Father.

Rule is *shepherd*. This is a reference to the Millennial reign of Christ in which the believers are to share. (Psalm 2:9)

Verse 28—And I will give him the morning star.

Christ is called "the bright and morning star" in Revelation 22:16. This refers to the Rapture of the Church—which was the hope of multitudes during the Dark Ages. Christ was their only light.

Verse 29—He that hath an ear, let him hear what the Spirit saith unto the churches.

The children of Jezebel will not hear, but the true children of the Lord Jesus will hear for the Spirit opens the blood-tipped ear.

Chapter 3

E. The Letter of Christ to the Church in Sardis—the Protestant Church—1517 A.D. to approximately 1800 A.D., 3:1-6

Sardis, the capital of Lydia, was one of the oldest and most important cities of Asia Minor. Well situated on a plain watered by the Pactolus river, it was the center of the carpet industry and was noted for its wealth. Coins were first minted here. The last prince was the wealthy Croesus, who was captured by Cyrus. Sardis was ruled by the Persians, Alexander, Antiochus the Great and finally by the Romans. It was destroyed by an earthquake during the reign of Tiberius.

The ruins of the temple of Cybele are still to be seen. The worship of the goddess Cybele resembled the corrupt worship of Diana of Ephesus. Recent excavations (summer of 1959) have been conducted at the site of ancient Sardis by a joint archaelogical expedition of Harvard-Cornell Universities. Many statue fragments dedicated to Roman deities were found, as were remains of chapels and a baptistry from the period of the early church. Recovered also were Greek urns, pots and other artifacts from 2000 B.C. to Islamic art of the time of Tamerlane.

Verse 1—And unto the angel of the church in Sardis write; These things saith he that hath the seven Spirits of God, and the seven stars; I know thy works, that thou hast a name that thou livest, and art dead.

The Lord Jesus presents Himself to this church as One having the seven spirits of God. This is the Holy Spirit whom Christ had sent into the world (John 16:7), even as the Father had sent Him into the world. For purposes of redemption Christ had become subject to the Father, and the Holy Spirit is subject to both the Father and the Son. Nevertheless, as to their positions in the Trinity they are equal.

During the dark night of the "Dark Ages" the Holy Spirit was still in the world doing the work that Christ had sent Him to do. The Reformation is the evidence of His presence and work.

The seven stars are the seven ministers. Christ still keeps His messengers and witnesses in the world.

Thy works is a word of commendation. This word is common to all periods with the exception of Smyrna and Pergamum—Smyrna was suffering and Pergamum was contending for the faith.

The Reformation recovered the doctrine of justification by faith, and this faith produced works (James 2:17-20). There is a second word of commendation in verse 4.

Thou hast a name that thou livest, and thou art dead, a frightful word of condemnation, is a picture of Protestantism. The great truths which were recovered in the Reformation have been surrendered by a compromising church. Although the great denominations and churches still repeat by rote the creeds of the church; in mind, heart and life they have repudiated them. Imposing programs, elaborate rituals, and multiplication of organizations have been substituted for the Word of God and real spiritual life. There is activity but no action, motion without movement, promotion without progress, and program without power. Although the outward form remains, the living creature has vacated the shell. A busy, hurried and exhausted church, leaving the main business undone, is a sorry substitute and cheap counterfeit for a church going forth in the fulness of the Spirit. Protestantism is dead, but instead of a funeral we are having a picnic. Dr. Harry Rimmer labeled the Sardis church, "The Dead Church."

Verse 2—Be watchful, and strengthen the things which remain, that are ready to die: for I have not found thy works perfect before God.

Wake up and watch out and establish the things that remain which were about to die, for I have found no works of thine fulfilled (perfected) before my God.

This is the second word of condemnation, directed as a word of warning to a lethargic and unanimated church (Romans 13:11, 12; I Thessalonians 5:4-6; I Peter 5:8). The danger is regression. That there is no spiritual progress "no works perfected" reveals that the Reformation was not a return to the apostolic church. Some of its doctrines were recovered: (1) the authority of the Word of God, (2) the total depravity of man, (3) justification by faith; yet there was practically no development of the Christian life, the church, nor of prophecy.

Other vestigial impediments of Romanism still clung to Protestantism—such as the sacraments, the clergy, and the building.

Verse 3—Remember therefore how thou hast received and heard, and hold fast, and repent. If therefore thou shalt not watch, I will come on thee as a thief, and thou shalt not know what hour I will come upon thee.

Remember means that Protestantism is to hearken back to the Reformation when all Europe was eager to hear and was stirred by the Word of God.

Thou hast received (perfect tense) means they had received the Word of God as a permanent deposit.

And heard (Aorist tense) means simply the act of hearing.

Hold fast means to *keep it.* Protestantism is losing what truth it recovered during the Reformation.

Repent is the repeated command of Christ to His Church.

If therefore thou shalt not wake up and watch, I will come as a thief (secretly), and thou shalt not know what hour I will come upon thee.

The city of Sardis had been captured twice, in its long history, through carelessness:

    (1) 549 BC.—a Median soldier scaled the parapet while the guard slept,

    (2) 218 B.C.—A Cretan likewise slipped over the wall while the sentries were careless.

Hence, this injunction of the Lord touched a tender spot in the memory of people of Sardis.

This is the warning of Christ to the Protestant church. Vincent calls particular attention to the word for thief. It is not the word used for a robber and plunderer, but emphasizes the idea of stealth and the unexpected. This is not a reference to the Second Coming of Christ but to His present coming in judgment (2:5 and 2:16). He uses many methods of exercising judgment in our day.

He does not come as a thief for His church (I Thessalonians 5:2-6).

Verse 4—Thou hast a few names even in Sardis which have not defiled their garments; and they shall walk with me in white: for they are worthy.

But thou hast a few names (persons) in Sardis that did not besmirch (defile) their Christian life (garments); and they shall walk with me in white (garments); for they are worthy.

Of Israel was a remnant; of the Church, a *few*—labeled by our Lord, "little flock." (Luke 12:32). Protestantism has its saints who love the Word, are faithful at the week-night service, and who work for the cause of Christ. They do not engage in sin-defiling activities. The defilement mentioned here comes from the mire and mud.

The *white garments* represent the faithful lives of Christians who merely reflect their identification and walk with Christ (Revelation 19:8, 14). Christ is the only righteousness of believers (Romans 3:21, 22).

A separated and faithful life still counts in the court of heaven.

Verse 5—He that overcometh, the same shall be clothed in white raiment; and I will not blot out his name out of the book of life, but I will confess his name before my Father, and before his angels.

The *overcomer* is the believer.

The *white raiment* is the righteousness of Christ (II Corinthians 5:21).

The book of the life is the literal rendering. Moses evidently referred to this Book in Exodus 32:32. The Psalmist refers to the same Book in Psalm 69:28.

Daniel, likewise, had reference to it in Daniel 12:1. In all of these Old Testament books the concept is not of a name being entered, but of a name being removed. Our Lord referred to the same Book in Luke 10:20. Paul refers to this Book in Philippians 4:3. Also the writer to the Hebrews makes mention of it in Hebrews 12:23. In all of these references the thought is that in the Book of Life in heaven the names are already inscribed.

In Revelation great importance is placed on this Book (see 13:8; 17:8; 20:12, 15; 21:27; 22:19). In these references the thought is that there are those whose names are recorded and those whose names are not recorded in the Book of Life.

Some identify the two books in Revelation 20:12 as the book of profession and the book of reality. They hold that names are erased from the book of profession but not from the book of reality.

Others have suggested that all names are placed in the Book of Life at the beginning, but some are removed. A person's lack of decision for or rejection of Christ causes his name to be removed at the time of death.

Both of these views propose serious objections as well as having good points to commend them. It is interesting to note that in the genealogies there are only two books which are identified:

(1) "The book of the generation of Adam" (Genesis 5:1), and

(2) "The book of the generation of Jesus Christ" (Matthew 1:1).

The phrase "the book of the generation" occurs in only these two places. The book of Adam is the book of death—"In Adam all die" (I Corinthians 15:22). The book of Jesus Christ is the Book of Life. Are the names of the entire human family inscribed in His Book, and are they erased at death if Christ has not been accepted?

Govett avoids either of these viewpoints by suggesting that there may be a temporary blotting out of the names. This seems to be an unsatisfactory explanation. However he makes the following helpful statement, "It seems certain (1) that the book of Life of the Apocalypse is but one. (2) And, that the name, to be blotted out, must first be enrolled there, is also certain."

I will confess his name . . . What grace to have Him confess us before the Father and the created intelligences of heaven!

Verse 6—He that hath an ear, let him hear what the Spirit saith unto the churches.

The call again is to those with a blood-tipped ear to hear the voice of the Spirit speaking through the Word of God.

F. The Letter of Christ to the Church in Philadelphia—The Revived Church—

from approximately the beginning of the 19th Century to the Rapture,
3:7-13

Philadelphia was located about 75 miles southeast of Sardis in Lydia. It was celebrated for its excellent wine—great vineyards covered the surrounding hills, and the head of Bacchus was imprinted on their coins. The city was built on four or five hills in a picturesque setting. Although this city had the longest duration of all seven cities, to whom letters were written, it was shaken frequently by earthquake. There is still a Turkish town at the site and the ruins of a pillar remain standing as a reminder of 3:12.

Verse 7—And to the angel of the church in Philadelphia write; These things saith he that is holy, he that is true, he that hath the key of David, he that openeth, and no man shutteth; and shutteth, and no man openeth;

The name *Philadelphia* means *brother love* (See Hebrews 13:1). This church exhibits the characteristics of the true Church even in its name (see I John 4:7-11).

Christ reminds them that He is *holy* holy at His birth (Luke 1:35), holy at His death (Acts 2:27) and holy in His present priestly office (Hebrews 7:26).

He is likewise true (John 1:9; 14:6; 15:1). *True* means genuine with an added note of perfection and completeness. Moses did not give the true bread: Christ is the true Bread. (John 6:32-35.)

He that hath the key of David (see Isaiah 22:22). This is different from the keys of hades and death (1:18). This speaks of His regal claims as the Ruler of this universe (Luke 1:32). He will sit on the throne of David in the Millennium, but today He is sovereign. That it is He who opens and closes (Matthew 28:18-20) is a comfort for us today.

Verse 8—I know thy works: behold, I have set before thee an open door, and no man can shut it: for thou hast a little strength, and hast kept my word, and hast not denied my name.

I know thy works: behold, I have given thee a door opened, which none can shut, for thou hast a little strength (dunamin), and didst keep my word, and didst not deny my name.

Addressed here is the "little flock" of believers in the days of cold formality and modern apostasy. He commends them on seven counts:

(1) *I know thy works* (see comment on 2:2).

(2) *Given thee a door opened, which none can shut* could be a door to the joy of the Lord or to a knowledge of the Scriptures. More likely it refers to a door of opportunity for witnessing and proclaiming the Word of God (compare Acts 19:9-10; I Corinthians 16:9).

(3) *Hast a little strength* (dunamin). This is a humble group of believers which doesn't have impressive numbers, buildings, and programs.

(4) *Didst keep my word* means that in a day when there is a denial of the inspiration of the Scriptures, this church believed the Bible to be authoritative. A twentieth century theologian, with leadership in the liberal ranks, stated that no intelligent person could believe in the verbal inspiration of the Bible.

(5) *And didst not deny my name* means that in a day when the deity of Christ is blatantly denied by seminary and pulpit, this church remained true to Him by proclaiming the God-man and His substitutionary death for sinners.

Verse 9—Behold, I will make them of the synagogue of Satan, which say they are Jews, and are not, but do lie; behold, I will make them to come and worship before thy feet, and to know that I have loved thee.

Behold I give of the synagogue of Satan, of them that say they are Jews, and are not, but lie. Behold, I will make them that they shall come and worship before your feet, and to know that I have loved you.

The remnant of Israel which was being saved had left the synagogue by this time and had given up the law as a means of salvation and sanctification (Romans 9:8; 11:5). Those who continued in the synagogue were now in a false religion. They were no longer true Jews.

Ignatius, according to Trench and reported by Vincent, refers to a local situation where converts from Judaism preached the faith they once despised. Saints will judge the world and angels (I Corinthians 6:2).

(6) Christ will make the enemies of the Philadelphian church to know that He loves this church. This is the sixth point of commendation.

Verse 10—Because thou hast kept the word of my patience, I also will keep thee from the hour of temptation, which shall come upon all the world, to try them that dwell upon the earth.

Because thou didst keep the word of my patience, I, also, will keep you out of (from) the hour of the trial, which is (about) to come upon the whole inhabited world to test (try) them that dwell upon the earth.

(7) The last commendation is that this church kept the Word of Christ in patience. This is evidently the patient waiting for the coming of Christ for His own (II Thes. 3:5). It has been in the present century that the doctrines of eschatology have been developed more than in all previous centuries combined. During the past twenty years there has been a revival of interest, in both Europe and America, relative to the second coming of Christ. Even liberals, while denying the literal character of it, have given it attention. The World

Council of Churches, meeting in Evanston, had the coming of Christ as its theme.

Christ's final word of encouragement to His Church is that it will not pass through the Great Tribulation. The Church is to be removed from the world (I Thessalonians 4:13-18), which is its comfort and hope (Titus 2:13). Such is the patient waiting of the Church "who through faith and patience inherit the promises." The Church is not anticipating the Great Tribulation with all its judgment (Revelation 13:1-8 and 11-17; John 5:24).

Verse 11—Behold, I come quickly: hold that fast which thou hast, that no man take thy crown.

This is the promise of Christ and hope of the Church. When He comes for His own, He will reward them (Revelation 22:12). It is possible for some enemy to rob a believer of his reward.

Verse 12—Him that overcometh will I make a pillar in the temple of my God, and he shall go no more out: and I will write upon him the name of my God, and the name of the city of my God, which is new Jerusalem, which cometh down out of heaven from my God: and I will write upon him my new name.

A pillar in the temple of my God speaks of a place and position of honor in heaven (Matthew 19:27-29; 20:23). The Church is a temple of living stones (Ephesians 2:19-22). A pillar denotes beauty, stability, and strength. The Church that had a little strength down here will have greater strength in heaven. This all speaks of permanence and honor.

And I will write upon him the name of my God, and the name of
the city of my God, the new Jerusalem (See Revelation 22:4).

Aaron wore a crown of gold which had engraven upon it, "Holiness to the Lord" (Exodus 28:36-38). This is the passport and visa of the believer which will enable Him, as a citizen of heaven, to pass freely upon this earth or anywhere in God's universe. He is a pillar to "go no more out," but with God's passport he is to go everywhere. Although this is paradoxical, it is all wonderful and blessedly true.

I will write upon him my new name (see note on 2:17). This is the new name of Christ for each believer.

All of this is in contrast to earth conditions where those in the Great Tribulation receive the mark of the beast in their foreheads (Revelation 13:17).

There is no word of condemnation of this church.

Verse 13—He that hath an ear, let him hear what the Spirit saith unto the churches.

He repeats again the final warning to each church. Only the Holy Spirit can open ears.

G. The Letter of Christ to the Church in Laodicea—The Apostate Church (The Contemporary Professing Church)—from approximately the time of the Philadelphian Church and continuing into the Tribulation, **3:14-22**

Laodicea was about 40 miles east and inland from Ephesus on the Lycus river. The name means "justice of the people" and was a popular woman's name among the Seleucidae of Syria. Also many towns bore this name. Laodicea was a place of great wealth, Greek culture, science, and literature. It boasted an excellent medical school. It was a center of industry with extensive banking operations. Here Cicero held court. Zeus (Jupiter) was the object of worship. The city was finally abandoned because of earthquakes. Remaining are extensive ruins among which are two Roman theaters, the stadium and three early Christian churches.

Verse 14—And unto the angel of the church of the Laodiceans write; these things saith the Amen, the faithful and true witness, the beginning of the creation of God.

And to the messenger of the church in Laodicea write; These things saith the Amen, the faithful and true witness, the beginning of the creation of God;

Amen—there is no reference to the vision of chapter one except the *amen*. This is the only place in Scripture where it is used as a proper name. In Isaiah 65:16 it should read, "the God of the amen." In Isaiah 7:9 the word *believe* is *amen*. This is the final message to the church and Christ is the One who alone will fulfill all that is spoken concerning the Church (II Corinthians 1:20).

Faithful and true witness reveals that Christ alone is the One who will reveal all and tell all. He speaks to the Church all that it should know. In this day of a compromising church it is well to have an authority to whom we can go in confidence.

The beginning of the creation of God. He speaks as Creator to an age that has accepted the evolutionary hypothesis (John 1:3; Colossians 1:16). Since He is the Creator He is likewise the Consumator. He will bring all things to pass in His own good time.

Verses 15, 16—I know thy works, that thou art neither cold nor hot: I would thou wert cold or hot. So then because thou art lukewarm, and neither cold nor hot, I will spue thee out of my mouth.

There is no word of commendation to this church. All is condemnation. Even the works are not called good works as they were in Thyatira. Here their works are marred by lukewarmness. Even the "good works" of this church are bad because of lack of reality.

Cold indicates one who is in active opposition to the church, fighting the Gospel of Christ.

Hot is the word for those with real spiritual fervor and passion like the original state of the Christians of Ephesus. (Romans 12:11)

Lukewarm. This is the only place in the Bible the word occurs.

Between these two positions are those who are lukewarm—who give the outward appearance of spiritual fervor but inwardly are as opposed to Christ as are those who are cold. Such is the state of many in fundamental circles who, though they profess to be sound in doctrine, by their lives they are denying Him. Such is hypocrisy of the worst kind. This word of condemnation, therefore, is more than a slight difference in the reading of a thermometer. It is a picture of spiritual zombis who lack life. It refers to religious racketeers who are minus reality.

Having a form of godliness, but denying the power thereof: from such turn away (II Timothy 3:5).

The picture is frightful and the effect upon Christ is worse. As lukewarm water is disgusting and sickening, He vomits these out of His mouth. They make Him sick.

Verse 17—Because thou sayest, I am rich, and increased with goods, and have need of nothing; and knowest not that thou are wretched, and miserable, and poor, and blind, and naked:

Thou sayest, I am rich, and have gotten riches, and have need of nothing; and thou doest not know that thou art the wretched one and miserable (the object of pity) and poor, and blind and naked.

This church made its boast of material possessions. Conversely the church in Smyrna was poor in material things—it was the church of slaves and poor folk. There were not many rich, not many noble.

For ye see your calling, brethren, how that not many wise men after the flesh, not many mighty, not many noble, are called (I Corinthians 1:26).

The present day church boasts of large membership, prominent people, huge attendance, generous giving, and ornate buildings.

A phenomenal growth in membership from 20 per cent of our population in 1884 to 35 per cent of the population in 1959 (61,000,000 Protestant church members) would indicate the possibility of a church on fire for God. And there are other indications:

Wealth beyond the wildest dreams of our forefathers—an income of $5 billion in 1959.

A building program that will see $800 million spent for new church structures.

Mass evangelistic meetings attended by tens of thousands.

Use of other mass media such as radio and literature increasing constantly.[1]

Worldly wealth is the measuring rod for the modern church. Spiritual values have been lost sight of or are entirely ignored. The church is not only rich in earthly goods, but it actually is in the business of accumulating wealth. People are urged to make their wills in favor of so-called Christian organizations. Radio programs and other professing Christian works are operated as promotional schemes to raise money to provide luxurious care for the promoters.

On the spiritual side of the ledger, the Laodicean church is *the wretched one*. It is worse off than any of the seven churches. It is to be pitied because it is spiritually poverty stricken. In it is no study of the Word, no love of Christ, and no witnessing of His saving grace—yet it is blind to its own true condition. It lacks the covering of the robe of righteousness.

Verse 18—I counsel thee to buy of me gold tried in the fire, that thou mayest be rich; and white raiment, that thou mayest be clothed, and that

[1] J. O. Percy, *Moody Monthly*

the shame of thy nakedness do not appear; and anoint thine eyes with eye-salve, that thou mayest see.

I counsel (advise) thee to buy of me gold refined by fire, that thou mayest become rich, and white garments that thou mayest clothe thyself, and the shame of thy nakedness be not made manifest; and eyesalve to anoint thine eyes that thou mayest see.

There is a note of irony that pervades this entire verse; yet it is the sincere invitation of the Saviour. Though this church has rejected His loving counsel, He offers it. He could command.

How can the bankrupt buy? The gold standard has been accepted by all nations. Christ wants to put this church on the spiritual gold standard. Although they think they are rich, they are bankrupt. He wants them to become truly rich. He wants them to be clothed with real righteousness (Romans 3:21-23; II Corinthians 5:21). He wants them taught by the Holy Spirit so that they can truly see (I Corinthians 2:9-10).

Verse 19—As many as I love, I rebuke and chasten: be zealous therefore, and repent.

In the Greek the emphasis is upon *I*. In this final word to the church, the Lord Jesus Christ asserts His authority. He rebukes (reproves) and chastens because of His love for the church. How many preachers today have the courage to rebuke their own congregations? How many congregations will accept rebuke?

Be zealous means to *be hot*. He is ordering this church to forsake it's lukewarm state.

Repent—this church needs repentance more than did all the others.

Verse 20—Behold, I stand at the door, and knock: if any man hear my voice, and open the door, I will come in to him, and will sup with him, and he with me.

This invitation seems detached from the message to Laodicea. It is a personal invitation sent out at the end of the age by the Lord Jesus who has been ignored and His claims rejected by the organized church. It is a gracious and personal invitation of our Lord. What loving condescension to come to the heart-door of sinners who ought instead to be knocking at His door—since they are the needy ones (Luke 11:5-10). He will not force His way in; the door must be opened from within. He respects the rights of His creatures.

His invitation is to the evening meal—the last call for dinner. It is an invitation to come to Him before the night of the Great Tribulation falls.

Verse 21—To him that overcometh will I grant to sit with me in my throne, even as I also overcame, and am set down with my Father in his throne.

As the Father's throne is shared by Christ, so Christ shares His throne with believers. They shall reign with Him.

The overcomer is the one who enters by faith into the victory of Christ (Romans 8:37).

Verse 22—He that hath an ear, let him hear what the Spirit saith unto the churches.

The final word and warning to the churches is to hear the still small voice of the Spirit speaking above the Babel of this world.

Thus concludes the earthly pilgrimage of the Church. The Church has been the theme of the past two chapters. Hereafter, the Church is no longer seen on earth. The subject changes and the scene shifts to heaven. Actually the Apocalypse begins at chapter four. Heretofore we have seen the introductory considerations.

We take you now by way of the Rapture to Heaven.

Chapters 4-22

INTRODUCTION

III. THE PROGRAM OF JESUS CHRIST—The Scene in Heaven.

(The Crisis in the World—the Coming of Christ—The Millennium—the Great White Throne—the New Heavens and the New Earth—the Eternal State)

As Revelation 1:19 gives the chronological division of the book, so 1:17,18 gives the Christological division of the book. "Things which must be hereafter" of 4:1 corresponds to "the things which shall be hereafter" of 1:19. Both are *meta tauta*—in the Greek, a change from this to an entirely different scene and subject. This section brings us to the last major division of the Revelation.

Several striking facts make it self-evident that we advance to a new division in chapter 4. The climate and conditions change radically.

(1) The Church is no longer seen in the world. Up to chapter 4 there have been nineteen references to the Church in the world. In fact, the subject of chapters 2 and 3 has been entirely devoted to the Church in the world. However, from chapter 4 to the end of the Revelation, the Church is never mentioned in connection with the world. The final and lone reference is a concluding testimony after the world's little day has ended (22:16). Christ said, "They are not of the world even as I am not of the world" (John 17:16). He also said, "I will come again, and receive you unto myself; that where I am, there ye may be also" (John 14:3).

(2) The scene shifts to heaven. Since the Church is still the subject, we follow it now to its new home—heaven. "How did the Church get to heaven?" is a good question. Paul gives the answer, "Caught up together with them in the clouds, to meet the Lord in the air." He defines the operation in I Corinthians 15:51, 52:

Behold, I shew you a mystery. We shall not all sleep, but we shall all be changed, in a moment, in the twinkling of an eye, at the last trump; for the trumpet shall sound, and the dead shall be raised incorruptible, and we shall be changed.

Faith places the sinner on the launching pad in the guided missile of the Church—from whence he shall go to meet the Lord in the air. The saints enter the opened door to heaven. The Church is with Christ: Christ is in heaven directing the events of the Great Tribulation.

(3) The Church is not a name but a definition of those who have trusted Christ in this age. "Church" is *Ecclesia* which means *"called out."* When the Church arrives at its destination, it loses the name by which it was known in the world: other terms are used to describe it.

We see the Church as twenty-four elders—representatives of the Church in heaven. We see also the Church in heaven as a bride.

The apostate organization, which bears the ecclesiastical terminology and continues on in the world, is not hereafter given the title of "church" but the frightful label of "the harlot".

(4) The judgments (begining at chapter six) would not be in harmony with the gracious provision and promise that God has made to the Church. If the Church remained in the world, it would frustrate the grace of God.

(5) Finally, to continue on from chapter 3 to chapter 4 without recognizing the break, is to ignore the normal and natural division in the book of Revelation as stated in 1:19. Only the scoffer can say, "All things continue as they were from the beginning of creation."

As this last division is entered with all of its judgment and wrath, it is well to keep in our perspective that Jesus Christ is central and is directing all events as He brings them to a successful and determined conclusion. There is "in the midst of the throne . . . a Lamb."

Chapter 4

THEME: The Church in Heaven with Christ, chapters 4-5

OUTLINE:

A. The Church in Heaven with Christ, chapter 4

    1. The Throne of God, 4:1-3

    2. The Twenty-Four Elders, 4:4,5

    3. The Four Living Creatures, 4:6-11

REMARKS:

The scene shifts from earth to heaven. It is a radical change. However, the Word of God describes personages and activities in heaven as normally as it described them on earth. There is no strain or involvement in superstition or mystery. The bridge over the great gulf is passed with ease and a reverent restraint. Only the Holy Spirit could describe things in heaven with as much ease as He describes things on the earth.

The Church is not seen under the familiar name it had in the world, but is now the priesthood of believers with the Great High Priest (Revelation 8:3). Heavenly scenes and creatures greet us in this section before our attention is drawn to the earth where, at the opening of the Great Tribulation, the four horsemen are to ride.

Christ is viewed in His threefold office of Prophet, Priest, and King—He is worshipped as God.

COMMENT:

    1. The Throne of God, 4:1-3

Verse 1—After this I looked, and, behold, a door was opened in heaven: and the first voice which I heard was as it were of a trumpet talking with me; which said, Come up hither, and I will shew thee things which must be hereafter.

After these things (meta tauta) I saw, and behold a door set open in heaven; and the first voice which I heard, a voice as of a trumpet speaking with me and saying, Come up hither, and I will shew thee the things which must come to pass after these things (meta tauta).

After these things both opens the verse and closes it. Repetition lends great emphasis and importance to this phrase. After "these (Church) things" of chapter 2 and 3, John is shown what follows the removal of the Church.

I saw is through the eye gate.

I heard is through the ear gate.

A door set open is one of the four "open doors" in the Revelation:

3:8—the door of opportunity and witness for Christ,

3:20—the open door of invitation of and identification with Christ,

4:1—the open door of translation and rapture of the Church,

40

19:11—the open door of the second coming and return of Christ.

John did not see this door opening as the Authorized Version suggests. This door was open all the time. It is the door through which believers have come to God for over 1900 years:

> Jesus saith unto him, I am the way, the truth, and the life: no man cometh unto the Father, but by me (John 14:6).

> I am the door: by me if any man enter in, he shall be saved, and shall go in and out, and find pasture (John 10:9).

We enter by faith. In modern teminology we might express it thus: faith puts us on the launching pad of the Church which is Christ, and at the Rapture we go through this door like a guided missile.

Come up hither is heaven's invitation to John and the *koinonia:*

> That which we have seen and heard declare we unto you, that ye also may have fellowship with us: and truly our fellowship is with the Father, and with his Son Jesus Christ (I John 1:3).

A voice as of a trumpet speaking introduces us to one of the simple symbols which occurs frequently from here on in Revelation. That it is a symbol is evident—a trumpet does not speak, in spite of what jazz addicts may say.

The voice was clear and commanding which reminds us of the account found in I Thessalonians 4:16, 17.

> For the Lord himself shall descend from heaven with a shout, with the voice of the archangel, and with the trump of God: and the dead in Christ shall rise first; then we which are alive and remain shall be caught up together with them in the clouds, to meet the Lord in the air: and so shall we ever be with the Lord.

Verse 2—And immediately I was in the spirit: and, behold, a throne was set in heaven, and one sat on the throne.

At once (straightway) I found myself in the Spirit: and, behold, a throne set in heaven, and one sitting on the throne.

At once denotes the brevity of time, which is one of the characteristics of the rapture (I Corinthians 15:51, 52).

In the spirit (see 1:10) indicates that the Holy Spirit is still guiding John into new truth and is showing him things to come (John 16:13).

A throne set in heaven gives us the place, and directs our attention to the center of attraction there. The throne represents the universal sovereignty and rulership of God (Psalm 11:4; 47:8; 97:2; 103:19; Ezekiel 1:26-28). It is the throne of God the Father and Jesus sits on His right hand (Psalm 110:1; Hebrews 1:3; 12:2). The Lord Jesus Christ is in charge of all events here. The throne of grace now becomes a throne of judgment.

Verse 3—And he that sat was to look upon like a jasper and a sardine stone: and there was a rainbow round about the throne, in sight like unto an emerald.

Our attention is directed to the One seated on the throne. Although He is God the Father, we should understand this to be the throne of the triune God. Nevertheless the three Persons of the Trinity are distinguished:

(1) God the Holy Spirit in verses 2 and 5,

(2) God the Father in verse 3,

(3) God the Son in 5:5.

John could distinguish no form of a person on the throne; only the brilliance and brightness of precious stones. God is a Spirit (John 4:24).

Jasper stone was the last stone identified in the breastplate of the High Priest (Exodus 28:20). It was first in the foundation of the New Jerusalem (Revelation 21:19). Also it was seen first in the wall of the New Jerusalem (Revelation 21:18). It was a many colored stone with purple predominating. Some identify it with the diamond.

Sardine stone is the sixth stone in the foundation of the New Jerusalem (Revelation 21:20). Pliny says it was discovered in Sardis from which it derived its name. In color it was a fiery red.

The first stone sets forth the holiness of God: the second the wrath or judgment of God. *Justice* is the watchword of this new order as *Grace* is of today.

Rainbow is the Greek word *iris*. It can mean halo. While the rainbow is polychrome, here it is emerald which is green (Ezekiel 1:28). After the judgment of the flood the rainbow appeared as a reminder of God's covenant to not destroy the earth again with a flood (Genesis 9:13-15). It appears here before the judgment of the Great Tribulation as a reminder that a flood will not be used in judgment. Green is the color of earth. The suggestion is that of Habakkuk: "In wrath remember mercy."

2. The Twenty-Four Elders, 4:4,5

Verse 4—And round about the throne were four and twenty seats: and upon the seats I saw four and twenty elders sitting, clothed in white raiment; and they had on their heads crowns of gold.

Our attention is next directed to the 24 thrones surrounding the throne of God. On these thrones are seated 24 elders *presbuterous*. Who are the elders? They are actual beings. Are these a new type of creatures to whom we are at this point introduced? David divided priests and Levites into 24 courses and placed 24 leaders over them (I Chronicles 24:4). The Church is a priesthood of believers. Elders were appointed in the churches to rule and represent the entire church (Titus 1:5). The Elders of verses 4 and 5 seem to us to be representative of the Church and therefore stand for the total Church from Pentecost to the Rapture.

White raiment is the righteousness of Christ (II Corinthians 5:21).

Crowns of gold indicates that the Church will rule with Christ (I Corinthians 6:3). Crowns are also given as rewards (James 1:12, I Peter 5:4; II Timothy 4:8).

Verse 5—And out of the throne proceeded lightnings and thunderings and voices: and there were seven lamps of fire burning before the throne, which are the seven Spirits of God.

The tense here is present—*proceed*. This makes vivid the dramatic action which is to take place.

Lightnings and thunderings always precede a storm in the midwest, and generally indicate the intensity of the storm. Here it occurs as a reminder that judgment is getting ready to break upon the earth as a storm.

Voices indicate that this is not a haphazard act of nature but the intelligent act of God.

Seven Spirits of God (see 1:4). This is a clear cut reference to the Holy Spirit. The Holy Spirit is no longer in the world to restrain evil and hold back judgment.

3. The Four Living Creatures, 4:6-11

Verse 6—And before the throne there was a sea of glass like unto crystal: and in the midst of the throne, and round about the throne, were four beasts full of eyes before and behind.

A sea of glass denotes the appearance and not the material. This sea is before the throne of God. This is another indication that the emphasis is not on mercy but on judgment. This sea represents the holiness and righteousness of God. (Hebrews 12:14; Matthew 5:8)

> To the end he may stablish your hearts unblameable in holiness before God, even our Father, at the coming of our Lord Jesus Christ with all his saints (I Thessalonians 3:13).

This placid sea indicates the position of rest to which the Church has come. No longer is she the victim of the storms of life:

> And He saith unto them, Why are ye fearful, O ye of little faith? Then He arose, and rebuked the winds and the sea; and there was a great calm (Matthew 8:26).

Four beasts are literally *four living creatures*—the Greek word is *zoa*. The emphasis is not upon the bestial but on the vital.

Full of eyes before and behind suggests alertness and awareness. These creatures, of the highest intelligence, are in God's presence. They resemble the cherubim of Ezekiel 1:5-10; 10:20 and the seraphim of Isaiah 6:2-3. Are they a new order of creatures in heaven that have not been revealed before in Scripture? The curtain is pulled back and we are looking into the very throne of God. We would expect to see what never before had been revealed. Godet states that they are not symbolic since they are not explained, but that they are representative.

Verse 7—And the first beast was like a lion, and the second beast like a calf, and the third beast had a face as a man, and the fourth beast was like a flying eagle.

First living creature was like a lion (Revelation 5:5) He communicates the office of Christ as king—as seen in the Gospel of Matthew.

Second living creature like a calf (ox) (Deuteronomy 25:4) The ox, the beast of burden and sacrifice, communicates here the office of Christ as servant—set forth in the Gospel of Mark.

Third living creature has a face as a man. He communicates the humanity of Christ—as emphasized in the Gospel of Luke.

Fourth living creature was like a flying eagle. (Exodus 19:4; Deuteronomy 32:11, 12.) He communicates the Deity of Christ—as seen in the Gospel of John.

These living creatures also represent the animal world as suggested by Godet:

Lion . . . wild beasts

Ox . . . domesticated animals

Eagle . . . birds

Man . . . head of all creation

(Note that there is no mention of fish. There is no more sea in the new earth, nor reptiles—since the serpent introduced sin. See Genesis 9:9-10 "fowl, cattle, and beast").

Verse 8—And the four beasts had each of them six wings about him; and they were full of eyes within: and they rest not day and night, saying, Holy, holy, holy, Lord God Almighty, which was, and is, and is to come.

Six wings corresponds to the seraphim of Isaiah 6:2.

Had should be *having*.

Holy holy, holy, Lord God Almighty is the refrain of the seraphim of Isaiah 6:3.

Which was, and is, and is coming refers to Christ (Revelation 1:8).

Verses 9-11—And when those beasts give glory and honour and thanks to Him that sat on the throne, who liveth for ever and ever. The four and twenty elders fall down before Him that sat on the throne, and worship Him that liveth for ever and ever, and cast their crowns before the throne, saying, Thou are worthy, O Lord, to receive glory and honour and power: for Thou hast created all things, and for thy pleasure they are and were created.

When is *whensoever*, indicating that this is a continual act of worship. Praise is the eternal activity of God's creatures. The creature worships the Creator as the triune God. (Worship is the activity of heaven. If you find worship boring down here, why do you want to go to heaven?)

The *crowns* of the Church are laid at Jesus' feet as an act of submission and worship.

Our Lord and our God is the full title of verse 11.

For thy pleasure is more accurately translated *because of thy will*, and *they were not and they were created* is the text of Manuscript B. God created them out of nothing.

Chapter 5

THEME: The Church in Heaven with Christ (continued), chapters 4-5

OUTLINE:

    4. Book with Seven Seals, 5:1-4

    5. Christ: the Lion of the Tribe of Judah and the Lamb which Has Been Slain, 5:5-10

    6. Myriads of Angels of Heaven Join the Song of Praise and Redemption, 5:11,12

    7. Universal Worship of the Saviour and Sovereign of the Universe, 5:13,14

REMARKS:

This chapter continues the same theme as the preceding one. The scene is set in heaven preparatory to the events of the Great Tribulation. The throne was the center of chapter four: the Lion and the Lamb, both of whom represent Christ, are the center of this chapter. He is both Sovereign and Saviour. He is in full charge of all events which follow in this book.

COMMENT:

4. Book with Seven Seals, verses 1-4

Verse 1—And I saw in the right hand of Him that sat on the throne a book written within and on the backside, sealed with seven seals.

And I saw on the right hand of Him that sat on the throne a book written within and on the back, close sealed (sealed tightly) with seven seals.

And shows that there should be no chapter division; the two sections belong together.

I saw—John is witness of these events.

God the Father holds in His hand a scroll which is rolled tightly and sealed closely with seven seals. Godet considers this "the book of the new covenant". Others label it the book of judgment. Walter Scott considers it "the Revelation of God's Purpose and Counsel Concerning the World". It perhaps should bear no title, as it is, as Dr. Ironside suggests, the title deed to this world. Compare Jeremiah 32:6-15 which is God's promise that God would bring His people back to their land.

Verse 2—And I saw a strong angel proclaiming with a loud voice, Who is worthy to open the book, and to loose the seals thereof?

Who has the right and title to this world? Who can rule it? Who can establish justice and righteousness?

Verse 3—And no man in heaven, nor in earth, neither under the earth was able to open the book, neither to look thereon.

No man of Adam's line has a right to it. Adam lost dominion through sin. Moses was the law giver but he was also a lawbreaker. David and his line failed. None of Adam's line qualifies. The Ruler must be a Redeemer. The Sovereign must be a Saviour.

45

Verse 4—And I wept much, because no man was found worthy to open and to read the book, neither to look thereon.

John enters into the drama because he has come from earth. The Revelation was written in tears. Is the earth to continue in sin and sorrow? Is there no future for this earth?

> And not only they, but ourselves also, which have the first fruits of the Spirit, even we ourselves groan within ourselves, waiting for the adoption, to wit, the redemption of our body (Romans 8:23).

Is no one competent to rule the earth? John is overwhelmed by the possibility that there may be no one.

> For we know that the whole creation groaneth and travaileth in pain together until now (Romans 8:22).

5. Christ, the **Lion** of the Tribe of Judah and the **Lamb** Which Has Been Slain, verses 5-10

Verse 5—And one of the elders saith unto me, Weep not: behold, the Lion of the tribe of Juda, the Root of David, hath prevailed to open the book, and to loose the seven seals thereof.

And one from among the elders saith unto me, Weep not: behold, the Lion of the tribe of Juda, the Root of David, hath overcome to open the book, and the seven seals thereof.

Evidently any one of the elders could have answered. They had spiritual illumination. This further identifies them as the Church:

> Henceforth I call you not servants; for the servant knoweth not what his lord doeth: but I have called you friends; for all things that I have heard of my Father I have made known unto you (John 15:15).

The Lord Jesus Christ is the only one who has right and title to this earth. He not only redeemed you and me, but He redeemed the earth. He is identified in this section in all His ministries that relate to the earth.

Lion of the tribe of Juda—see Genesis 49:9.

Root of David—see II Samuel 7:16, 25; 23:5; Isaiah 11:1-12. The Lord Jesus Christ has the right to rule, as He is the fulfillment of the prophecies made in the Old Testament relative to the future of the world. All of those prophecies will be fulfilled at His second coming.

Verse 6—And I beheld, and, lo, in the midst of the throne and of the four beasts, and in the midst of the elders, stood a Lamb as it had been slain, having seven horns and seven eyes, which are the seven Spirits of God sent forth into all the earth.

John is still a spectator to this scene.

A Lamb is in the diminutive: it is literally "a little lamb"—denoting its gentleness and its willingness to be sacrificed. (Isaiah 53:7)

As it had been slain indicates the redemptive and vicarious substitutionary death of Christ. The emphasis is upon the fact that He was slain with violence.

Stood is rather *standing*. It speaks of His resurrection. He is no longer seated at the right hand of God (Psalm 110:1).

He is *in the midst of the throne*—indicating that He is before the throne and ready to act as the righteous judge.

Seven horns denotes perfect power (a horn speaks of power, compare Daniel 7, 8)—He is omnipotent.

Seven eyes denotes perfect knowledge—He is omniscient.

He moves in the fulness of the Spirit who is the Spirit of wisdom and understanding. (Isaiah 11:2)

The Lion character refers to His Second Coming:	The Lamb character refers to His First Coming:
The Lion Speaks of His majesty	The Lamb speaks of His meekness
As Lion He is Sovereign	As Lamb He is Saviour
As Lion He is Judge	As Lamb He is judged
The Lion speaks of the government of God	The Lamb speaks of the grace of God.

Verse 7—And he came and took the book out of the right hand of him that sat upon the throne.

Took is correctly *hath taken*. He moves to the throne through the Tribulation. He judges the world in righteousness before He reigns in righteousness.

He is no longer the Intercessor of the Church, for the Church is now with Him. He is beginning to act as Judge. The movement here is important.

Verse 8—And when he had taken the book, the four beasts and four and twenty elders fell down before the Lamb, having every one of them harps, and golden vials full of odours, which are the prayers of saints.

When He took the book (aorist tense)—This is the great movement of all creation. Notice the worship of the Lamb by the four living creatures and the 24 elders (the Church).

The *harp* denotes praise. The elders do not play on the harps.

Four and twenty elders act as priests. Only the Church is a priesthood of believers in heaven. Carl Armeding gives this arresting thought, The Prayer of Christ for believers is answered in the elders (John 17).

(1) That they might know Him

(2) That they might be with Him

(3) That they might behold His glory.

Vials full of odours is more accurately *bowls full of incenses*—identified as the prayers of the saints. The golden altar of incense in the tabernacle presents the same picture (Leviticus 16:12,13; Psalm 141:2).

Verses 9-10—And they sung a new song, saying, Thou art worthy to take the book, and to open the seals thereof: for thou wast slain, and hast redeemed us to God by thy blood out of every kindred, and tongue, and people, and nation; and hast made us unto our God kings and priests: and we shall reign on the earth.

And they sing a new song, saying, Worthy art thou to take the book and to open the seals of it: for thou wast slain and didst purchase unto God in thy

47

blood (men) of every tribe, tongue, people, and nation, and madest them unto our God a kingdom and priests, and they shall reign on the earth.

They indicates that both living creatures and elders sing this song. The angelic hosts join the Church in praise.

Sing (present tense) denotes the continuation of praise.

Praise is directed to the Lamb with the Book. He is praised now as the Redeemer of men in all ages and all races.

New song is the song of redemption. The old song is the song of creation (Job 38:7, compare Rev. 4:11).

Worthy reveals that He now fills the entire horizon of praise and worship. He is the only One worthy of praise. They sing of His shed blood in heaven. Down here many denominational churches are taking from their hymn books all songs about the blood of Christ, but the blood is not being taken out of the hymn books in heaven—they sing about the blood.

The change of pronoun from *us* to *them* is important. They are praising the Lamb for those yet to be saved on the earth—the Tribulation saints.

A kingdom and priests refer to the Tribulation saints. The Church will not reign *on* the earth but *over* the earth.

6. Myriads of **Angels of Heaven Join the Song** of Praise and Redemption, verses 11, 12

Verses 11-12—And I beheld, and I heard the voice of many angels round about the throne and the beasts and the elders: and the number of them was ten thousand times ten thousand, and thousands of thousands; saying with a loud voice, Worthy is the Lamb that was slain to receive power, and riches, and wisdom, and strength, and honour, and glory, and blessing.

And I saw, and I heard a voice of many angels round about the throne and the living creatures and the Lamb, and the number of them was ten thousands of ten thousands (myriads), and thousands of thousands, saying with a great voice, Worthy is the Lamb that hath been slain to take the power, and riches, and wisdom, and might, and honor, and glory, and blessing.

I saw and I heard is John's constant reminder that he is a spectator to this scene in heaven. As far as I could see, John said, there was an infinite number of angels out there praising the One who had taken the seven sealed book.

Many angels round about the throne shows that the circle in heaven is ever widening. A circle larger than the 24 elders now joins the heavenly chorus. The number of them is fantastic. This is a heavenly host which, as the stars, no man can number. Daniel saw this same scene. (Daniel 7:10).

They praise Christ as Redeemer. The Lamb that yielded to the insults of depraved men now receives the adoration of all the heavenly host.

The power is important to note, for all the other attributes accorded to the Lamb belong in this one package labeled: THE POWER.

Riches—all spiritual and material wealth. He has a surplus of everything.

7. **Universal Worship** of the Saviour and Sovereign of the Universe, verses 13-14

Verses 13-14—And every creature which is in heaven, and on the earth,

and under the earth, and such as are in the sea, and all that are in them, heard I saying, Blessing, and honour, and glory, and power, be unto him that sitteth upon the throne, and unto the Lamb for ever and ever. And the four beasts said, Amen. And the four and twenty elders fell down and worshipped him that liveth for ever and ever.

Every animate creature of God joins in this universal act of worship both in heaven and earth. Evidently the animals in the earth and the fish in the sea join in this volume of praise.

The *living creatures* add their amen. The Church here can only fall down in silent adoration and praise.

Chapter 6

THEME: The opening of 6 seals of the book with 7 seals.

OUTLINE:

B. THE GREAT TRIBULATION IN THE WORLD, chapters 6-18

1. **Opening of the Seven-Sealed Book,** chapters 6-8:1

   a. Opening of the **First** Seal, verses 1, 2
      (Rider on a White Horse)

   b. Opening of the **Second** Seal, verses 3, 4
      (Rider on a Red Horse)

   c. Opening of the **Third** Seal, verses 5, 6
      (Rider on a Black Horse)

   d. Opening of the **Fourth** Seal, verses 7, 8
      (Rider on a Pale Horse)

   e. Opening of the **Fifth** Seal, verses 9-11
      (Prayer of the Martyred Remnant)

   f. Opening of the **Sixth** Seal, verses 12-17
      (The Day of Wrath Has Come—Beginning the Last Half of the Great Tribulation)

REMARKS:

This chapter brings us to the opening of the period which our Lord labeled "The Great Tribulation." It is synonymous with and simultaneous to the 70th week of Daniel. Daniel, chapter 9 and Matthew, chapters 24 and 25 cover this period. The bulk of the book of Revelation, chapters 6-18, is concerned with this period. There is a multiplying of judgment and intensification of wrath in this section.

7 SEALS—chapters 6-8:1

7 TRUMPETS—chapter 8:2-11

7 STARTLING PERSONS—chapters 12, 13
Woman, Satan, Man Child
Michael, Remnant of Israel
Beast out of the Sea, Beast out of the Earth

7 BOWLS OF WRATH—chapters 15, 16

BURDEN OF BABYLON—chapters 17, 18

Babylon, at the Tower of Babel, represents the first organized rebellion against God (Genesis 11:1-9). Babylon represents the last rebellion against God, both religiously and politically. When Babylon falls, earth's last vestige of rebellion by man against God is crushed. Satan's final effort to organize the rebellion of Gog and Magog (Revelation 20:7-9) is both meaningless and fruitless.

It is essential to keep before us that this book is the manifestation of Jesus Christ. He is no longer walking among the lampstands, for they all have been removed from this earth. He is no longer the High Priest standing as Intercessor, but is now the Executor of God's will upon the earth as He opens the seals of the book. All of the judgments of the Great Tribulation usher forth from the seals out of which come the Trumpets, Persons, and Bowls.

The Great Tribulation is triggered from heaven. Jesus Christ directs the entire operation. Chapters 4 and 5 were but the preparation for that which was to follow—the judgment on the earth.

Chapter 4—the Throne; the triune God

Chapter 5—the Book; the Lord Jesus Christ

Certain factors are brought into focus which increase the intensity and ferocity of the Great Tribulation.

(1) The Holy Spirit restrains evil no longer,

(2) The true Church, as light and salt, is removed,

(3) The devil knows he has but a short time,

(4) Evil men are free to carry out their nefarious plans, e.g., the Antichrist,

(5) There is direct judgment from God (verse 17).

It should be emphasized that the Great Tribulation does not break suddenly like a great tornado. The opening of the seals is gradual, logical and chronological. They are opened one at a time.

The first four which send forth the four horsemen, represent four great cosmic events which penetrate the entire social structure in every continent and race. These are revolutionary global movements.

God assumes responsibility for calling forth the judgments of the horsemen. Such was His method in the Old Testament (II Kings 8:1; Isaiah 7:18, 19).

COMMENT:

a. Opening of the **FIRST** Seal, verses 1, 2

(Rider on the White Horse)

Verses 1, 2—And I saw when the Lamb opened one of the seals, and I heard, as it were the noise of thunder, one of the four beasts saying, Come and see. And I saw, and behold a white horse: and he that sat on him had a bow; and a crown was given unto him: and he went forth conquering, and to conquer.

And I saw when the Lamb opened one of the seven seals, and I heard one of the four living creatures saying as a sound of thunder, Go. And I saw, and behold a white horse, and one sitting on him having a bow, and a crown was given to him, and he went out conquering, and to conquer.

The Lord Jesus Christ has now taken the book with seven seals and He begins to break the seals *ad seriatum*. He is in full charge and every creature in heaven is moving at His command. The four horsemen ride only after He breaks the seals and issues the order. The Authorized Version gives the impression that there is an invitation given to John, *Come and see*. However, since *see* should be omitted and since the order issues from heaven, the proper translation is *Go*.

It is restated by John that he *saw* and *heard*.

To determine the symbolism of .the rider on the white horse, has given rise to a difference of opinion. The preponderate interpretation among commentators is that he represents Christ, using Psalms 45 and Revelation 19 in support of this position (see Govett and Newell, etc.).

Most of the contemporary Bible expositors, as well as some in the past, consider the rider on the white horse as Antichrist (see Scott, Ironside, Chafer, Walvoord, Woodbridge, and Pentecost).

This latter view seems to meet the demands of the text more completely. When Christ comes on a white horse, as in Revelation 19, the Millennium follows; this rider initiates the Great Tribulation—not the Millennium.

We believe the rider to be "the little horn" of Daniel 7, the Man of Sin, the Beast of Revelation 13, the ruler of the restored Roman Empire, and the final world dictator. He comes to power by ushering in a false peace.

Professor A. J. Toynbee, Director of Studies in the Royal Institute of International Affairs, says,

> By forcing on mankind more and more lethal weapons and at the same time making the whole world more and more inter-dependent economically, technology has brought mankind to such a degree of distress that we are ripe for deifying any new Caesar who might succeed in giving the world unity and peace.

> For when they shall say, Peace and safety; then sudden destruction cometh upon them, as travail upon a woman with child; and they shall not escape (I Thessalonians 5:1).

G. K. Chesterton observes,

> One of the paradoxes of this age is that it is the age of Pacifism, but not the age of Peace.

In a recent news item, we read of a woman in Fayetteville, Arkansas, who named the United Nations as the beneficiary to her $700,000 estate "in the fervent hope that this relatively small contribution may be of some effect in bringing about universal peace on earth and good will among men."

The Ford Foundation, the world's wealthiest private organization, having listed resources of $492,678,255, has announced that the money eventually will be used to work for world peace and better government, living and education conditions.

The world will think that it is entering the Millennium when it is actually entering the Great Tribulation. The Great Tribulation comes in like a lamb but it goes out like a lion.

This rider could not be Christ, in view of the fact that Christ is the Lamb in the midst of the throne who, as the Lion of the Tribe of Judah, the Root of David, is directing the earthly events from heaven and is giving the orders to the four horsemen to ride. Christ is clearly identified in Revelation 19, while here the identity is obscure. That, itself, is suggestive that it is not Christ but an imitation of Him.

b. Opening of the **SECOND** Seal, verses 3,4
(Rider on a Red Horse)

Verses 3, 4—And when he had opened the second seal, I heard the second beast say, Come and see. And there went out another horse that was red: and power was given to him that sat thereon to take peace from the earth, and that they should kill one another: and there was given unto him a great sword.

And when He opened the second seal, I heard the second living creature saying, Go. And another horse, fiery red (flame colored) went out. And there was given to the one sitting on him to take peace from the earth, and that they should kill (violently) one another, and there was given to him a great sword.

The *peace* which the rider on the white horse brought to the earth was temporary and counterfeit. The Antichrist presents himself as a ruler who brings peace to the world—but he cannot guarantee it, for God says there is no peace to the wicked.

After the white horse of peace, there rides forth the *fiery red horse* of war. The greatest global conflict takes place in the Great Tribulation, culminating in the final phase of the Battle of Armageddon when the Lord Jesus rides forth to the earth to establish His kingdom.

Peace is not only taken from the earth but the *great sword* is symbolic of the frightful slaughter which takes place during this period of the Great Tribulation.

John states that he not only heard but that he saw the first horsemen. While it is stated here that he only heard the order for the second horseman to go forth, it must be assumed that he also saw him. John uses the word *another* in connection with this horse and not with the other three which seems to indicate that the first two horses are vitally linked together. Peace and war belong together here—to emphasize further the false peace which introduces the Great Tribulation.

The insane desire of the world today for peace at any price is fertile soil for a counterfeit Christ to sow his propaganda of peace and good will.

c. Opening of the **THIRD** Seal, verses 5, 6

Verses 5, 6—And when he had opened the third seal, I heard the third beast say, Come and see. And I beheld, and lo a black horse; and he that sat on him had a pair of balances in his hand. And I heard a voice in the midst of the four beasts say, A measure of wheat for a penny, and three measures of barley for a penny; and see thou hurt not the oil and the wine.

And when he had opened the third seal, I heard the third living creature saying, Go. And I saw, and behold a black horse, and the one sitting on him having a balance (scales) in his hand. And I heard a voice in the midst of the four living creatures say, a choenix (a quart) of wheat for a denarius, and three choenix (quarts) of barley for a denarius; and do not hurt the oil and the wine.

The color of the *black horse* speaks of mourning (Jeremiah 4:28, Malachi 3:14 "mournfully in black") and famine (Lamentations 4:8, 9; 5:10). The *balance* indicates a scarcity of food.

The historian Herodotus says that a choenix (quart) of corn was a soldier's daily supply of food. A denarius was a day's wage (Matthew 20:2). A working man would be unable to support his family in that day.

The oil and wine are luxuries enjoyed by the rich. Oil would correspond to our toiletries, beauty aids and body conditioners. The wine corresponds to the liquor that will be in abundance.

It is difficult for those of us who live in a land of abundance, surplus and super-markets to visualize such scarcity; yet even today most of the world's population go to bed with an empty stomach.

Way back in 1798 the Rev. Thomas Malthus concluded that "the power of population is indefinitely greater than the power of the earth to produce subsistence for man." The prediction had little weight in his day. In 1959 the U.N.'s 77-nation Food and Agriculture Organization met in Rome to talk about "the fight against hunger and malnutrition." At this meeting Toynbee declared: "Sooner or later food production will reach its limit. And then, if population is still increasing, famine will do the execution that was done in the past by famine, pestilence and war combined."

Sir John Boyd Orr, Director-General of the U.N. Food and Agricultural Organization warns, "I shall finish my office by giving a last warning to the world. If it is not solved there will be world chaos in the next fifty years. The nations of the world are insane."

"There are today 750 million people getting hungrier in countries bordering the Communist sphere." There are some "fifteen countries where the population is out-running the food supply" (Calgary Herald).

In Germany, since World War II, 10 million refugees escaped from behind the iron curtain, and have come through Berlin. In Greece 80% of the people exist on an income of less than 30c a day. The poverty of Egypt and Arab countries has been increased by the entrance of 1 million refugees. India underdeveloped and overpopulated, has been always a land of want. Recently 3 million refugees from Pakistan and Tibet have increased the misery. Calcutta is called "the human Dead Sea." In Hong Kong a million refugees have swelled the population to the second heaviest concentration per square mile in the world. There are 110,000 "squatters" on housetops; others sleep and die on sidewalks. In Cuba, at our own front door, thousands, since the revolution, have lost their homes and are destitute.

Famine always follows war. Many can recall the conditions in Europe immediately following World Wars I and II which existed even in our day of glorious abundance. In the Tribulation such conditions will be intensified. When the red horse of war rides, the black horse of famine will be riding on his heels.

d. Opening of the **FOURTH** Seal, verses 7, 8
(Rider on a Pale Horse)

Verses 7, 8—And when he had opened the fourth seal, I heard the voice of the fourth beast say, Come and see. And I looked, and behold a pale horse: and his name that sat on him was Death, and Hell followed with him. And power was given unto them over the fourth part of the earth, to kill with sword, and with hunger, and with death, and with the beasts of the earth.

And when He had opened the fourth seal, I heard the voice of the fourth living creature saying, Go. And I looked and behold a pale (greenish-yellow) horse; and the one sitting upon him, Death was his name; and Hades followed with him. And there was given unto them authority over the fourth part of the earth, to kill with the sword, and with famine, and with death (pestilence), and by the (wild) beasts of the earth.

Death is no more personalized here than is war—although the rider is given the name of *death*. There is more involved in physical death than meets the eye, for a human being is more than physical and death is more than cessation of physical activity. While death takes the body, hades is the place where the spirit of a lost man goes (Luke 16:23 ASV).

A literal translation of Romans 5:14 reads thus:

And nevertheless death became king from Adam down to Moses, even over them who did not sin after the fashion of Adam's sin (transgression) who is the type of Him (The Adam) who was to come (The Coming One).

Paul personifies death here as he does sin in the two preceding verses for emphasis. Sin and death entered the world at the same time. Death is the result of sin. During the interval from Adam to Moses, men did not commit the same sin as did Adam nor was their sinning a transgression of a law as was Adam's. Nevertheless, Adam's sin became their sin for they died as Adam died. Even babies died in the flood.

Death here evidently is all inclusive and embraces all phases.

(1) Physical death—this refers only to the body. It comes to man because of Adam's sin.

(2) Spiritual death—separation from and rebellion against God. We inherit this dead nature from Adam.

(3) Eternal death—eternal separation from God. Unless man is redeemed this inevitably follows. This is the second death of Revelation 20:14.

Adam is definitely declared here to be a type of Christ. Death must be laid at Adam's door as his total responsibility. God did not create man to die. It was a penalty imposed because Adam transgressed God's command. His transgression is our transgression and his death is our death. Thus Christ is the head of a new creation. This new creation has life in Him. He is totally responsible for their life and eternal bliss.

Dr. I. S. Chafer adds this statement, "Thus spiritual death comes mediately through an unbroken line of posterity. Over against this, physical death is received from Adam immediately, as each person dies in body because of his own personal share in Adam's first sin."

During the Great Tribulation *death* will ride unbridled:

And except those days should be shortened, there should no flesh be saved: but for the elect's sake those days shall be shortened (Matthew 24:22).

At the Great White Thone death is finally destroyed (Revelation 20:14). This is confirmed by Paul, "The last enemy that shall be destroyed is death" (I Corinthians 15:26). John reasserts it, "And God shall wipe away all tears from their eyes; and there shall be no more death, neither sorrow, nor crying, neither shall there be any more pain: for the former things are passed away (Revelation 21:4).

The *sword, famine, pestilence,* and *wild beasts* will decimate by one fourth the population of the earth.

> For thus saith the Lord GOD: How much more when I send my four sore judgments upon Jerusalem, the sword, and the famine, and the noisome beast, and the pestilence, to cut off from it man and beast (Ezekiel 14:21)?

The *pale horse* represents plague and pestilence that will stalk the earth. It also encompasses the possibility of germ warfare.

Dr. Frank Holtman, head of the University of Tennessee bacteriological department, has made this statement:

> While the greater part of a city's population could be destroyed by an atomic bomb, the bacteria method might easily wipe out the entire population within a week. The virus causing psittacosis or parrot fever, one of the most deadly of human diseases, is appraised by the scientists as being the most preferable for this purpose. While the cost of producing psittacosis bombs is comparatively cheap, its lethal potency is extremely high. According to Thomas R. Henry, science editor, less than one cubic centimeter of this virus is required to infect 20 million human beings when released in the air as infinitesimal spray.

It is the concensus of our leaders that the four horsemen are getting ready to ride. They do not call them horsemen—they call them war, famine and disease.

e. Opening of the **FIFTH** Seal, verses 9-11
(Prayer of the Martyred Remnant)

Verses 9, 10—And when he had opened the fifth seal, I saw under the altar the souls of them that were slain for the word of God, and for the testimony which they held: and they cried with a loud voice, saying, How long, O Lord, holy and true, dost thou not judge and avenge our blood on them that dwell on the earth?

And when He opened the fifth seal, I saw under the altar of burnt sacrifice the souls (psuchas) of those slain on account of the Word of God, and on account of the witness which they had; and they cried with a great voice, saying, How long (until when) O Master, the Holy and True, dost Thou not judge and avenge our blood on them that dwell on the earth (earth dwellers)?

The *altar* is in heaven, and is evidently where Christ offered His blood for the sins of the world (see author's book, *The Tabernacle, God's Portrait of Christ*).

> It was therefore necessary that the patterns of things in the heavens should be purified with these; but the heavenly things themselves with better sacrifices than these. For Christ is not entered into the holy places made with hands, which are the figures of the true; but into heaven itself, now to appear in the presence of God for us (Hebrews 9:23, 24).

The *souls* mentioned here are Old Testament saints, redeemed by the blood of Christ. The fact that they do not have their redeemed bodies, indicates that they did not participate in the rapture of the Church (I Thessalonians 4:13-18). They are the martyred saints from Abel to John the Baptist (Genesis 4:10).

That the blood of all the prophets, which was shed from the foundation of the world, may be required of this generation; from the blood of Abel unto the blood of Zacharias, which perished between the altar and the temple: verily I say unto you, It shall be required of this generation (Luke 11:50, 51).

They rest upon Old Testament ground and plead for justice on the basis of God's holy law.

Verse 11—And white robes were given unto every one of them; and it was said unto them, that they should rest yet for a little season, until their fellow-servants also and their brethren, that should be killed as they were, should be fulfilled.

And there was given to them to each one a white robe; and it was said to them, that they should rest (in peace) yet for a little time until their fellow servants also, and their brethren who should be killed even as they were, should be fulfilled.

These Old Testament saints are clothed in the righteousness of Christ, and have the peace of God in their lives. They are to wait until the Tribulation saints are martyred and join them. The location is heaven where they are waiting to come with Christ to the earth.

f. Opening of the SIXTH Seal, verses 12-17
(The Day of Wrath Has Come—Beginning the Last Half of the Tribulation)

Verses 12, 13—And I beheld when he had opened the sixth seal, and, lo, there was a great earthquake; and the sun became black as sackcloth of hair, and the moon became as blood; and the stars of heaven fell unto the earth even as a fig tree casteth her untimely figs, when she is shaken of a mighty wind.

And I saw when He opened the sixth seal, and there was a great earthquake; and the sun became black as sackcloth of hair, and the whole moon became as blood; and the stars of heaven fell into the earth, as a fig tree casteth her unripe figs when she is shaken of a great wind.

These phenomena in the physical realm are to be taken literally. Great cosmic disturbances indicate that the great Day of God's Wrath has come. Only God can control the forces of nature. At the crucifixion and resurrection of Christ there were earthquakes (Matthew 27:51; 28:2). The Great Tribulation both opens and closes with these upheavals in the natural universe:

(1) Beginning of the Tribulation—Joel 2:30 31 compare with Acts 2:20,
(2) End of the Tribulation—Joel 3:9-17; Isaiah 13:9-13; 34:1-4; Matthew 24:29.

In our day, earthquakes are on the increase. There is barely a moment when the seismographs of the world are not recording a disturbance somewhere. In a recent earthquake in Fukui, Japan, it is reported that 2,850 were instantly killed, and 30,450 houses totally destroyed. The atom bomb left Hiroshima with thirteen buildings standing, but Fukui has only three. Everythng else is charred wreckage or is still burning.

Professor R. A. Daly, in *Our Mobile Earth*, writes, "In the last 4,000 years earthquakes have caused the loss of 13,000,000 lives, and far the most awful earth-shock is yet to come. 'And there was a great earthquake, such as there was not since there were men upon the earth, so great an earthquake, so mighty; and the cities of the nations fell' (Rev. 16:18)."

At the time of the writing of these notes, word has come of great earthquakes in Chile, South America, accompanied by tidal waves and the eruption of many active volcanoes in the immediate area. The total waves caused damage as far away as the west coast of the United States, Hawaii, and Japan.

Verse 14—And the heaven departed as a scroll when it is rolled together; and every mountain and island were moved out of their places.

And the heaven was removed as a scroll when it is rolled up, and every mountain and island were moved out of their places.

This verse is to be taken literally. The effect of atomic explosions demonstrates the possibility of this (see Nahum 1:5). This event will be repeated at the Great White Throne Judgment described in Revelation 20:11.

Verses 15-17—And the kings of the earth, and the great men, and the rich men, and the chief captains, and the mighty men, and every bondman, and every free man, hid themselves in the dens and in the rocks of the mountains; and said to the mountains and rocks, Fall on us, and hide us from the face of him that sitteth on the throne, and from the wrath of the Lamb: for the great day of his wrath is come; and who shall be able to stand?

And the kings of the earth and the princes, and the chief captains, and the rich, and the strong, and every bondman and free man hid themselves in the caves and rocks of the mountains. And they say to the mountains and to the rocks, Fall on us and hide us from the face of the One sitting on the throne, and from the wrath of the Lamb, for the Great Day of their wrath came, and who is able to stand?

What is worse than an atomic bomb, a hydrogen bomb or a germ bomb? This is it—the wrath of God. The upheaval in nature which introduces the Great Day of Wrath, alarms to the same extent the men of the world. Society is disrupted and civilization is revolutionized and shaken. Men in every rank and from all walks of life are affected. None escapes. The events in nature strike terror to the hearts of all.

The *wrath of the Lamb* is a paradoxical phrase. The gentleness of a lamb is proverbial. Men speak today of the gentle Jesus whom, they feel, would never punish sin. The philosophy of our day is that all will be well and everybody will eventually arrive in heaven. However, at the beginning of the Great Tribulation the entire thinking of man is changed. They will know that the Lamb sends judgment—He who was slain for their sins and has been rejected by them.

At the end of the Great Tribulation when again nature is in turmoil, these men, hardened as was Pharaoh, attempt actual war against the Lamb (Revelation 19:19).

How can anyone survive these events? Civilians will not escape and civil defense will not avail. Chapter seven answers the question which closes this chapter, *Who shall be able to stand?*

Nevertheless, God precedes judgment with grace. Today God is gracious, and we do not realize how wonderful is that grace. God is holy, and to be in His presence with your sin on you would be worse than a bomb exploding in your face. In Christ we are made acceptable. Not one of us can stand in God's presence unless we are clothed in the righteousness of Christ.

Chapter 7

THEME: God seals a remnant of Israel, and saves a redeemed company of Gentiles during the Great Tribulation.

OUTLINE:

g. **Interlude,** chapter 7

(1) **Reason** for the Interlude Between the 6th and 7th Seals, verses 1-3

(2) **Remnant** of Israel Sealed, verses 4-8

(3) **Redeemed** Multitude of Gentiles, verses 9-17

REMARKS:

A format is followed from the breaking of the Seals to the Bowls of Wrath. Between the sixth and seventh of each, there is an interlude in which extra information is given concerning persons and events. The seventh of each leads into the next series of seven in logical procession.

Before the opening of the seventh and last seal, there is an interlude to make sure of the salvation of a great company of people—after the Church is removed, and before the Great Tribulation breaks with all its ferocity and intensity. This is probably the last three and one half years.

The Great Tribulation is a time in which a great company will turn to God.

COMMENT:

(1) **Reason** for the Interlude Between the 6th and 7th Seals, verses 1-3

Verse 1—And after these things I saw four angels standing on the four corners of the earth, holding the four winds of the earth, that the wind should not blow on the earth, nor on the sea, nor on any tree.

After this I saw four angels standing on the four corners of the earth, holding firmly the four winds of the earth, that no wind might blow on the earth nor on the sea, nor on any tree.

These four angels are agents of God who are active during the Great Tribulation. They hold back the physical winds of nature, which are judgments of God upon the earth, until the two great companies of the redeemed are sealed and made secure. This is the lull before the breaking of the storm. In chapter 8 the storm breaks in all its fury.

The wind fulfills the will of God:

> Fire, and hail; snow, and vapour; stormy wind fulfilling his word (Psalm 148:8).

The word for *earth* is *ges*. It seems to indicate the ungodly world which is left on earth after the Rapture of the Church.

Verses 2, 3—And I saw another angel ascending from the east, having the seal of the living God: and he cried with a loud voice to the four angels, to whom it was given to hurt the earth and the sea, saying, Hurt not the earth, neither the sea, nor the trees, till we have sealed the servants of our God in their foreheads:

And I saw another angel ascending from (the) sunrising, having (the) seal of (the) Living God, and he cried with a great voice to the four angels, to whom it had been given to hurt the earth and the sea, saying, Hurt not the earth, nor the sea, nor the trees, until we shall have sealed the servants (bond slaves) of our God, in their foreheads.

Another angel is a fifth angel with a higher rank than the four—for he gives them orders.

A great voice is in the Greek *phone megale*. When the two words are reversed, it is megaphone, which gives us an idea of the character of the voice.

With frightful and fearful judgment ready to break upon the earth, it is necessary to secure the servants of God—to preserve them from the wrath of Satan (see Revelation 12:13-17).

For then shall be great tribulation, such as was not since the beginning of the world to this time, no, nor ever shall be. And except those days should be shortened, there should no flesh be saved: but for the elect's sake those days shall be shortened (Matthew 24:21, 22).

Exactly what is the seal in the forehead, cannot be asserted. Though Scripture does not describe it, it evidently is in contrast to the mark of the beast (Revelation 13:16, 17).

(2) **Remnant** of Israel Sealed, verses 4-8

Verse 4—And I heard the number of them which were sealed: and there were sealed an hundred and forty and four thousand of all the tribes of the children of Israel.

And I heard the number of those sealed, a hundred and forty and four thousand, sealed out of every tribe of the children of Israel.

This company can be identified without speculation. They number 144,000 which is a literal number that need not be spiritualized to mean another number. This is the believing remnant of Israel. In all ages, from the time of Abraham, God has had a remnant among these people (see Ezekiel 6:8; Isaiah 1:9).

That is, They which are the children of the flesh, these are not the children of God: but the children of the promise are counted for the seed (Romans 9:8).

But what saith the answer of God unto him? I have reserved to myself seven thousand men, who have not bowed the knee to the image of Baal. Even so then at this present time also there is a remnant according to the election of grace (Romans 11:4, 5).

This remnant is composed of servants who shall proclaim the Gospel of the Kingdom during the Great Tribulation.

And this gospel of the kingdom shall be preached in all the world for a witness unto all nations; and then shall the end come (Matthew 24:14).

They will evangelize the world by preaching the death, resurrection and return of Christ. Through their ministry, a great company of Gentiles will turn to God.

The 144,000 are further identified as Israelites by the twelve-tribe division.

The same number from each tribe indicates their equality before God in grace, mercy and service.

Verses 5-8—Of the tribe of Juda were sealed twelve thousand. Of the tribe of Reuben were sealed twelve thousand. Of the tribe of Gad were sealed twelve thousand. Of the tribe of Aser were sealed twelve thousand. Of the tribe of Nephtalim were sealed twelve thousand. Of the tribe of Manasses were sealed twelve thousand. Of the tribe of Simeon were sealed twelve thousand. Of the tribe of Levi were sealed twelve thousand. Of the tribe of Issachar were sealed twelve thousand. Of the tribe of Zabulon were sealed twelve thousand. Of the tribe of Joseph were sealed twelve thousand. Of the tribe of Benjamin were sealed twelve thousand.

Of the tribe of Judah were sealed twelve thousand; of the tribe of Reuben twelve thousand; of the tribe of Gad twelve thousand; of the tribe of Asher twelve thousand; of the tribe of Naphtali twelve thousand; of the tribe of Manasseh twelve thousand; of the tribe of Simeon twelve thousand; of the tribe of Levi twelve thousand; of the tribe of Issachar twelve thousand; of the tribe of Zebulun twelve thousand; of the tribe of Joseph twelve thousand; of the tribe of Benjamin were sealed twelve thousand.

In this listing of the twelve tribes, there are several peculiarities to recognize. First, the word for seal is not repeated after each tribe as the Authorized Version has it. It is used with only the tribe of Judah at the beginning, and the tribe of Benjamin at the end.

Judah heads the list, supplanting the tribe of Reuben, whose right to that position had been forfeited by Reuben's sin. Judah was the tribe given pre-eminence (Genesis 49:8-10). Out of Judah, Christ himself came.

The tribes of Dan and Ephraim are omitted from this list. Both of these tribes were guilty of going into idolatry (Deuteronomy 29:18-21).

(1) Dan— the first tribe that fell into idolatry (Judges 18:30), was for centuries one of the headquarters of that calf-worship whereby "Jeroboam made Israel to sin" (I Kings 12:28-30). Given top priority in the Millennium (Ezekiel 48) indicates that it will be preserved during the Great Tribulation without being sealed—which reveals the greater grace of God.

Levi takes the place of Dan in the count of those sealed. Ordinarily the priestly tribe was not numbered with the other tribes. During the Great Tribulation they will be numbered among the evangelists.

(2) Ephraim—was also guilty of idolatry (Hosea 4:17). The 10 northern tribes of Israel were sometimes corporately designated as *Ephraim,* for this tribe was the leader. Ephraim was the tribe which led in the division of the kingdom (I Kings 11:26).

Joseph takes the place of Ephraim—obviously his name is substituted for that of his son.   However, Ephraim's place is restored during the Millennium (Ezekiel 48:5).

(3) **Redeemed** Multitude of Gentiles, verses 9-17

Verses 9-10—After this I beheld, and, lo a great multitude, which no man could number, of all nations, and kindreds, and people, and tongues, stood before the throne, and before the Lamb, clothed with white robes, and palms in their hands; and cried with a loud voice, saying Salvation to our God which sitteth upon the throne, and unto the Lamb.

After these things I saw, and behold, a great multitude which no man could number, out of every nation and out of tribes, and peoples, and tongues, standing before the throne and before the Lamb arrayed (clothed) in white robes and palm branches in their hands; and they cry with a great voice saying, The salvation to our God, who sitteth on the throne and to the Lamb.

The size of this multitude is stupendous. It is not a one-man-job to number them. These are Gentiles who have been saved during the Great Tribulation. The greatest days of God's salvation are in the future. These converts will come from every corner of the earth. All nations, tribes and languages are represented. These are Gentiles—in contrast to the 144,000 who are Israelites.

Standing before the throne and before the Lamb indicates that they are redeemed, a fact which their song confirms.

White robes typify the righteousness of Christ with which they are clothed.

Palm branches is literally *palm trees,* a sign of their victory in Christ. This multitude forms a part of the real Triumphal Entry when Christ returns to the earth. The Gentiles will observe the feast of Tabernacles during the Millennium (Zechariah 14:16, 17).

Verses 11, 12—And all the angels stood round about the throne, and about the elders and the four beasts, and fell before the throne on their faces, and worshipped God, saying, Amen: Blessing, and glory, and wisdom, and thanksgiving, and honour, and power, and might, be unto our God for ever and ever. Amen.

And all the angels were standing around the throne, and about the elders and the four living creatures; and they fell before the throne on their faces, and worshipped God, saying, Amen, blessing, and glory, and wisdom, and thanksgiving, and honor, and power, and might, be unto our God for ever and ever. Amen.

This is a stupendous scene of universal worship of God by His creatures, joining the great company of Gentiles saved during the Great Tribulation.

Notice that these creatures praise God for His attributes and goodness, but not for salvation—they are sinless creatures, not redeemed sinners.

Verses 13, 14—And one of the elders answered, saying unto me, What are these which are arrayed in white robes? and whence came they? And I said unto him, Sir, thou knowest. And he said to me, These are they which came out of great tribulation, and have washed their robes, and made them white in the blood of the Lamb.

And one of the elders answered, saying unto me, These which are arrayed in the white robes, who are they, and whence came they? And I say unto him, My Lord, thou knowest. And he said to me, These are they which came out of the Great Tribulation, and they washed their robes, and made them white in the blood of the Lamb.

John, quizzed by one of the elders, is unable to identify this great company. If they had belonged to the Church, John would have recognized them: if they were Old Testament saints or Israelites, John would have known. This company he does not recognize.

They are identified as redeemed Gentiles, who have come out of the Great Tribulation, redeemed by the blood of Christ.

God has only one way of saving mankind—that is by faith in the death and resurrection of Christ.

Moreover, brethren, I declare unto you the gospel which I preached unto you, which also ye have received, and wherein ye stand; by which also ye are saved, if ye keep in memory what I preached unto you, unless ye have believed in vain. For I delivered unto you first of all that which I also received, how that Christ died for our sins according to the scriptures; and that he was buried, and that he rose again the third day according to the scriptures (I Corinthians 15:1-4).

In whom we have redemption through his blood, the forgiveness of sins, according to the riches of his grace (Ephesians 1:7).

This great company is not part of the Church. We need to enlarge our conceptions of the redeemed to extend beyond the borders of the Church.

Verses 15-17—Therefore are they before the throne of God, and serve him day and night in his temple: and he that sitteth on the throne shall dwell among them. They shall hunger no more, neither thirst any more; neither shall the sun light on them, nor any heat. For the Lamb which is in the midst of the throne shall feed them, and shall lead them unto living fountains of waters: and God shall wipe away all tears from their eyes.

Therefore are they before the throne of God, and serve Him day and night in His temple (sanctuary); and He that sitteth on the throne shall spread His tabernacle (tent) over them. They shall hunger no more, neither thirst any more; neither shall the sun strike upon them, nor any heat (scorching wind): for the Lamb in the midst of the throne shall be their shepherd, and shall guide them into fountains of waters of life; and God shall wipe away every tear from their eyes.

This great company is further identified here as to their place of service. They serve in the temple of God—there is no temple connected with the Church either here or hereafter. These are more of *the other sheep.* Believers of today need to recognize that there are redeemed companies other than the Church.

These believers, having passed through the horrors of the Great Tribulation, undoubtedly have experienced the very things from which, it is said here, they are finally delivered. They have known hunger, thirst, the force of the elements and convulsions of nature, which transpire during the Great Tribulation.

Chapter 8

THEME: The opening of the 7th seal, introducing the 7 angels blowing 7 trumpets (the first 4 trumpets are in this chapter).

OUTLINE:

  h. Opening of the Seventh Seal—Introduction of Seven Trumpets, 8:1

2. Blowing of the **Seven Trumpets,** chapters 8:2-11:19
  a. Angel at the Altar with Censer of Incense, 8:2-6
  b. **First** Trumpet—Trees Burnt, 8:7
  c. **Second** Trumpet—Seas Became Blood, 8:8, 9
  d. **Third** Trumpet—Fresh Water Becomes Bitter, 8:10, 11
  e. **Fourth** Trumpet—Sun, Moon, Stars Smitten, 8:12, 13

REMARKS:

After the parenthetical matter of the sealing of the two companies in chapter 7, the opening of the seals is resumed. Only the 7th seal remains to be opened. The opening of the 7th seal introduces the 7 angels with the 7 trumpets. This sets the pattern for a remainder of the book of Revelation. Before the 7th of any series is introduced, a subsidiary subject is introduced to provide more light on the particular series.

The 7 trumpets bring us to the full intensity of the Great Tribulation. The 7 seals bring judgments which are the natural results of the activities of sinful man apart from God. The 6th seal brings the judgments of nature. The 7 trumpets reveal that God is judging directly and supernaturally a rebellious race. The first four series of sevens can be explained in the following manner:

(1) Seven Seals—judgment which is the result of man's wilful activity,

(2) Seven trumpets—judgment which is the direct activity of God,

(3) Seven Personalities—judgment which is the result of Satan's fight against God,

(4) Seven Vials (Bowls)—final judgment of the Great Tribulation, which is the direct activity of God because of man's and Satan's rebellion.

There is a strange and strong similarity between the plagues of Egypt, in Moses' day, and the trumpet judgments. It is both reasonable and logical to conclude that if one is literal, the other is likewise literal. These are literal plagues of the Great Tribulation. It is well to keep in mind that this is a revelation of Jesus Christ. These are not hazy and shadowy symbols which can be dissipated into thin air by some specious system of hermeneutics. When symbols are used—and they are used in this book—the key is supplied. Scripture will furnish the explanation. Revelation is the last book in the Bible, because a knowledge of the 65 books preceding it is the basic requirement for an understanding of its vivid language (II Peter 1:20).

COMMENT:

h. Opening of the Seventh Seal—Introduction of Seven Trumpets, verse 1

Verse 1—And when he had opened the seventh seal, there was silence in heaven about the space of half an hour.

And when (ever) He opened the seventh seal there came to pass silence in heaven of about a half hour.

The Lord Jesus Christ is still in command. When He opens the seventh seal, there is introduced a fanfare of seven trumpets. He directs the action from heaven.

First of all, He orders a halt on all fronts—heaven, hell, and earth. Nothing can move without His permission. He had already ordered the cessation of natural causes on earth when He ordered the sealing and saving of two definite groups (7:1). Now for a brief moment there is a lull in judgment activity. There is a heavenly hush. Godet defined it, "This silence is a pause of action." Why this strange silence? His patience is not exhausted. When the 6th Seal was opened and nature responded with a mighty convulsion, brave men weakened for a moment. Christ gave them opportunity to repent, but like Pharaoh of old, when the heat was taken off, his wilful heart returned to its original intention; so these men go back to their blasphemous conduct when there is a calm. They probably rebuke themselves for showing a yellow streak. After all, it was only nature reacting—everything can be explained by natural causes.

This is the lull before the storm. Someone has said, "The steps of God from mercy to judgment are always slow, reluctant, and measured." God is reluctant to judge, for He is slow to anger. Judgment is His strange work:

> For the LORD shall rise up as in mount Perazim, he shall be wroth
> as in the valley of Gibeon, that he may do his work, his strange
> work; and bring to pass his act, his strange act (Isaiah 28:21).

God "hath no pleasure in the death of him that dieth." This silence marks the transition from Grace to Judgment.

2. Blowing of the **Seven Trumpets,** chapters 8:2-11:19

a. Angel at the Altar with Censer of Incense, 8:2-6

Verse 2—And I saw the seven angels which stood before God; and to them were given seven trumpets.

And I saw the seven angels who stand before God, and there was given to them seven (war) trumpets.

The seven angels introduce us to a special group whom we evidently should have met before. Apparently, Gabriel is one of these angels, as he so identified himself to Zacharias when he announced the birth of John the Baptist. The seraphim are also identified as beings who stand before God (see Isaiah 6:1, 2). However, these seven angels are seemingly a different order than seraphim, as their mission and service is different.

Seven trumpets have a special meaning for Israel. God gave instructions to Moses for making two silver trumpets. Two was the number of witness. On the wilderness march they were used for a twofold purpose: (1) "the calling of the assembly," (2) "the journeying of the camps."

> Make thee two trumpets of silver; of a whole piece shalt thou make
> them: that thou mayest use them for the calling of the assembly, and
> for the journeying of the camps (Numbers 10:2).

When Israel entered the land, the trumpets were used for two other purposes:

> And if ye go to war in your land against the enemy that oppresseth you, then ye shall blow an alarm with the trumpets; and ye shall be remembered before the LORD your God, and ye shall be saved from your enemies. Also in the day of your gladness, and in your solemn days, and in the beginnings of your months, ye shall blow with the trumpets over your burnt offerings, and over the sacrifices of your peace offerings; that they may be to you for a memorial before your God: I am the LORD your God (Numbers 10:9, 19).

A single trumpet was blown, on the wilderness march, to assemble the princes.

> And if they blow but with one trumpet, then the princes, which are heads of the thousands of Israel, shall gather themselves unto thee (Numbers 10:4).

This corresponds to the "last trump" which is blown at the Rapture of the Church:

> Behold, I shew you a mystery; We shall not all sleep, but we shall all be changed, in a moment, in the twinkling of an eye, at the last trump: for the trumpet shall sound, and the dead shall be raised incorruptible, and we shall be changed (I Corinthians 15:51, 52).

> For the Lord himself shall descend from heaven with a shout, with the voice of the archangel, and with the trump of God: and the dead in Christ shall rise first (I Thessalonians 4:16).

The trumpet sounded an alarm, which moved Israel on the wilderness march. An alarm sounded to move each division. The tribes were divided into four groups of three tribes each, which camped on all four sides of the Tabernacle. The Levites were divided into three separate families, Kohath, Gershon, and Merari. The alarm was blown seven times to get Israel through the wilderness and into Palestine. The Seven Trumpets of Revelation will likewise have the positive effect of moving Israel into the land. After the 7th trumpet, Israel is identified for us, in chapter 12, as the special object of God's protection.

An understanding of the trumpets will prevent us from identifying the last trump of the Church with the seventh trumpet of the Revelation.

As the trumpets of Israel were used at the battle of Jericho, so the walls of this world's opposition to God will crumble and fall during the Great Tribulation.

Verse 3—And another angel came and stood at the altar, having a golden censer; and there was given unto him much incense, that he should offer it with the prayers of all saints upon the golden altar which was before the throne.

And another angel came and stood over (epi) the altar, having a golden censer (bowl); and there was given unto him much incense, that he should add it unto (give it unto) the prayers of all the saints upon the golden altar which was before the throne.

Another angel is positively not Christ. Christ is no longer in the position of an intercessor. He now holds the book of seven seals (having just opened the 7th Seal), as He directs all the activities from the throne. This angel is, as stated, just another angel who does Christ's bidding.

The *golden altar* is the place where prayer was offered.

Incense is likened unto prayer. David said, "Let my prayer be set before thee as incense" (Psalm 141:2). Incense speaks of the value of Christ's name and work in prayer. "If ye ask in my name" was His injunction. The incense was given to this angel—Christ needed nothing given to Him. The prayers of the saints, which were offered under the Fifth Seal (Revelation 6:9-11), are now being answered because of the person and sacrifice of Christ.

Verse 4—And the smoke of the incense, which came with the prayers of the saints, ascended up before God out of the angel's hand.

And the smoke of the incense, with the prayers of the saints, went up before God out of the angel's hand.

Prayer is answered because of Christ.

Verse 5—And the angel took the censer, and filled it with fire of the altar, and cast it into the earth: and there were voices, and thunderings, and lightnings, and an earthquake.

And the angel hath taken (takes) the censer, and filled it with the fire of the altar, and he throws (casts) it upon (into) the earth: and there were (came to pass) thunders, and voices, and lightnings, and an earthquake.

The High Priest took a censer of incense as he carried the blood into the Holy of Holies. Here the ritual is reversed. The censer is hurled upon the earth —rather than waved before God. The earth, having rejected the death of Christ for the judgment of their sins, must now bear the judgment upon their own sins.

Thunders denote the approach of the coming storm of God's judgment (see Revelation 4:5).

Voices reveal that this is the intelligent direction of God and not the purposeless working of natural forces.

Lightnings follow the thunder. This is not a reversal of the natural order. We see the lightning before we hear the thunder, due to the fact that light waves move faster than sound waves.

Earthquake is earth's response to the severe pressure which will be placed upon it.

Verse 6—And the seven angels which had the seven trumpets prepared themselves to sound.

And the seven angels having the seven trumpets prepared themselves that they should blow the trumpets.

This is a solemn moment. The half-hour of silence is over. The prayers of the saints have been heard. The order is issued to prepare to blow. The angels come to attention. At the blowing of the trumpets, divine wrath is visited upon rebellious men. The blowing of the trumpets does not introduce symbols or secrets—the plagues are literal.

b. FIRST Trumpet—Trees Burnt, verse 7

Verse 7—The first angel sounded, and there followed hail and fire mingled with blood, and they were cast upon the earth: and the third part of trees was burnt up, and all green grass was burnt up.

And the first (blew the trumpet) sounded, and there followed hail and fire, mingled in blood, and they were cast into the earth and the third part of the earth was burnt up, and the third part of the trees was burnt up, and all the green grass was burnt up.

Judgment falls upon all plant life from the grass to the great trees. Every form of botanical life is affected first. Fire, the great enemy, is the instrument. The forests and prairies, covered with grass, are partially destroyed by fire. One third of the earth denotes the wide extent of the damage—and it means one third, not one fourth. Plant life was the first to be created, and it is first to be destroyed (see Genesis 1:11, 12).

This is a literal judgment upon plant life in the same way that the 7th plague on Egypt was literal (see Exodus 9:18-26). The plague on Egypt was local, while here in the Tribulation it is global.

c. SECOND Trumpet—Seas Become Blood, verses 8, 9

Verses 8, 9—And the second angel sounded, and as it were a great mountain burning with fire was cast into the sea: and the third part of the sea became blood; and the third part of the creatures which were in the sea, and had life, died; and the third part of the ships were destroyed.

And the second angel sounded (blew the trumpet), and as it were a great mountain burning with fire was thrown (cast) into the sea, and the third of the sea became blood; and there died the third of the creatures which were in the sea died, (even) they that have life. And the third of the ships was destroyed.

The sea, which occupies most of the earth's surface, is next affected by the direct judgment of God. The separation of land and sea occurred on the same day in which plant life appeared (see Genesis 1:9, 10).

John does not say that a burning mountain was cast into the sea, but rather a great mass or force—*as it were a great mountain.* This careful distinction in the use of language should be noted, especially since it is the common practice to lump together everything in this book and call it symbolic. The mountain represents something as literal and tangible as that indicated in Jeremiah 51:25:

> Behold, I am against thee, O destroying mountain, saith the LORD, which destroyest all the earth: and I will stretch out mine hand upon thee, and roll thee down from the rocks, and will make thee a burnt mountain.

This literal mass falls in the literal sea and one third becomes literal blood and one third of all the literal living creatures in the literal sea die a literal death. Nothing could be plainer. Also, one third of the literal ships of all literal nations are literally destroyed.

d. THIRD Trumpet—Fresh Waters become Bitter, verses 10, 11

Verses 10, 11—And the third angel sounded, and there fell a great star from heaven, burning as it were a lamp, and it fell upon the third part of the rivers, and upon the fountains of waters; and the name of the star is called Wormwood: and the third part of the waters became wormwood; and many men died of the waters, because they were made bitter.

And the third angel blew the trumpet (sounded), and a great star burning as a torch fell from (out of) heaven, and it fell upon the third part of the rivers, and upon the fountains of the waters; and the name of the star is called Wormwood (Apsinthos); and the third part of the waters became wormwood; and many men died of the waters, because they were made bitter.

Fresh *water* is polluted under the third trumpet, and the drinking-water for mankind is contaminated. Those of us who live in Southern California know something of the scarcity of fresh water for drinking and domestic use. In Dallas, Texas, during the drought of the '50's, the water supply of the city, in man-made lakes, was exhausted. It was necessary to get water from Red River, into which the oil companies had let drain salt water from their deep wells. The drinking-water was so salty that it was barely possible to drink it. Many people traveled to the surrounding little towns to get a bottle of water to bring home. From these experiences, we learn how dependent mankind is upon fresh water.

In Exodus 15:23-25, the children of Israel came to Marah, where they found bitter waters. Moses was directed to a tree which, when cast into the waters, made them sweet. Here in Revelation the sweet waters are made bitter by a meteor. The tree speaks of the cross of Christ.

Wormwood is a name used metamorphically in the Old Testament, according to Vincent, in the following ways:

(1) Idolatry of Israel (Deuteronomy 29:18),
(2) Calamity and sorrow (Jeremiah 9:15; 18:15; Lamentations 3:15, 19),
(3) False judgment (Amos 5:7).[1]

The star is literal and is a meteor containing poison, which contaminates one third of the earth's fresh water supply. The name suggests that this is a judgment upon man for idolatry and injustice. Calamity and sorrow are the natural compensation.

e. **FOURTH** Trumpet—Sun, Moon, Stars Smitten, verses 12, 13

Verse 12—And the fourth angel sounded, and the third part of the sun was smitten, and the third part of the moon, and the third part of the stars; so as the third part of them was darkened, and the day shone not for a third part of it, and the night likewise.

And the fourth angel blew the trumpet (sounded), and the third part of the sun was smitten, and the third of the moon, and the third of the stars; in order that a third part of them might be darkened, and the day not shine for the third part of it, and the night in like manner.

Another phase of creation, on which mankind is solely dependent for light and life, is the sun. To a lesser degree, man is dependent on the moon and stars.

It was on the fourth day of re-creation that these heavenly bodies appeared, the light from them breaking through the firmament to the earth.

And God said, Let there be lights in the firmament of the heaven to divide the day from the night; and let them be for signs, and for seasons, and for days, and years: and let them be for lights in the firmament of the heaven to give light upon the earth: and it was so. And God made two great lights; the greater light to rule the day, and

---

[1] M. R. Vincent, Word Studies in the New Testament, vol. 2, p. 506.

the lesser light to rule the night: he made the stars also (Genesis 1:14-16).

These were to be for signs and seasons.

Our Lord indicated that in the Great Tribulation, there would be special signs in these three heavenly bodies:

> Immediately after the tribulation of those days shall the sun be darkened, and the moon shall not give her light, and the stars shall fall from heaven, and the powers of the heaven shall be shaken (Matthew 24:29).

> And there shall be signs in the sun, and in the moon, and in the stars; and upon the earth distress of nations, with perplexity; the sea and the waves roaring (Luke 21:25).

The laws of nature are radically altered by these disturbances. There is a definite limitation—only a third of the light and of the day is affected. The intensity of light has the wattage reduced by one third. Apparently the reason it is not completely blotted out is due to God's covenant with Noah and the race:

> While the earth remaineth, seedtime and harvest, and cold and heat, and summer and winter, and day and night shall not cease (Genesis 8:22).

A statement from Govett is intensely interesting in this connection—in view of present day efforts to eliminate the death penalty:

> Hence day continues still, though its brightness is diminished. God shows His right to call in question man's right to the covenant. He has not kept the terms. Blood for blood is not shed by the nations. By this time the command to put the murderer to death is, through a false philanthropy, refused by the world.[2]

Under these first four trumpets the expression *one third* has been used 12 times. This is not coincidental or accidental, but is the scriptural use of the divine number of God's government dealing with the earth. There were 12 tribes of Israel and 12 apostles who are to sit on 12 thrones judging the 12 tribes of Israel.

It is well to note the significance of Psalm 46, especially the first 3 verses:

> God is our refuge and strength, a very present help in trouble. Therefore will not we fear, though the earth be removed, and though the mountains be carried into the midst of the sea; though the waters thereof roar and be troubled, though the mountains shake with the swelling thereof.

Verse 13—And I beheld, and heard an angel flying through the midst of heaven, saying with a loud voice, Woe, woe, woe, to the inhabiters of the earth by reason of the other voices of the trumpet of the three angels, which are yet to sound!

And I saw and heard one eagle, flying in mid-heaven (the meridian), saying with a great voice (phone megale), Woe, woe, woe to them dwelling upon the earth, by reason of the remaining voices of the trumpet of the three angels who are about to blow the trumpet (sound).

---

[2] Robert Govett, The Apocalypse Expounded, p. 180.

Under the fourth trumpet the solemn announcement is made of a peculiar intensity of woe and judgment in connection with the last three trumpets. It is a warning to those who dwell upon the earth to prepare for the stepping-up of the judgments.

It is *one eagle* rather than *an angel* who makes the announcement. The eagle is used in the Old Testament as a symbol of God's grace:

> Ye have seen what I did unto the Egyptians, and how I bare you on eagles' wings, and brought you unto myself (Exodus 19:4).

The eagle is also a symbol of His judgment:

> The LORD shall bring a nation against thee from far, from the end of the earth, as swift as the eagle flieth; a nation whose tongue thou shalt not understand (Deuteronomy 28:49).

> Set the trumpet to thy mouth. He shall come as an eagle against the house of the LORD, because they have transgressed my covenant, and trespassed against my law (Hosea 8:1)

This eagle speaks. If a parrot and parakeet can be taught by man to speak, God will have no difficulty in making an eagle speak. This is quite literal.

The comment of Govett, at this point, is very pertinent and timely:

> But this eagle not only flies, but *speaks*. Is that literal or symbolic? If any think it is not absurd to suppose that an eagle may be made to speak, as Balaam's ass was, let him take it literally. If this is beyond his faith, let him take it symbolically. It is, I trust, the only case in which he will find his faith so tried.[3]

Finally, it is interesting to note that our Lord used the eagle to speak of His coming:

> For wheresoever the carcase is, there will the eagles be gathered together (Matthew 24:28).

³ Govett, op. cit., 180, 181

Chapter 9

THEME: The blowing of the fifth and sixth trumpets, a fallen star and the loosing of the four angels at the Euphrates River.

OUTLINE:

f. **FIFTH** Trumpet—**Fallen Star** and Plague of **Locusts**, verses 1-12

g. **SIXTH** Trumpet—**Angels Loosed** at River Euphrates, verses 13-21

REMARKS:

The last three trumpets are marked off from the other four by identification with the three woes (8:13; 9:12; 11:14). These woes mark the deepest darkness and most painful intensity of the Great Tribulation. This is generally associated with the last part (3½ years), the blackest days in human history.

The language used in this section is admittedly the most difficult of interpretation. This does not preclude our policy of following the literal line, even when the figures adopted are the most vivid and wild. If another interpretation is proper, John will furnish us the key.

COMMENT:

f. **FIFTH** Trumpet—**Fallen Star** and Plague of **Locusts**, verses 1-12

Verse 1—And the fifth angel sounded, and I saw a star fall from heaven unto the earth: and to him was given the key of the bottomless pit.

And the fifth angel sounded (blew the trumpet), and I saw a star out of heaven fallen into the earth, and there was given to him a key of the long shaft (pit, well) of the abyss.

There is some disagreement as to the identification of this fallen star. This star is different from the stars mentioned at the sounding of the fourth trumpet. This star acts with intelligence. He is given a key which he uses—no inanimate star could do this. We believe that this star is Satan. Some identify the star with Antichrist. If so, this lends support to the view that Antichrist is Satan incarnate. Reasons for interpreting this star as Satan are abundant.

How art thou fallen from heaven, O Lucifer, son of the morning! how art thou cut down to the ground, which didst weaken the nations! (Isaiah 14:12).

And he [Jesus] said unto them, I beheld Satan as lightning fall from heaven (Luke 10:18).

And no marvel; for Satan himself is transformed into an angel of light (II Corinthians 11:14).

These Scriptures abundantly confirm the position that Satan is in view here. John will state later that Satan was put out of heaven and cast to the earth (see Revelation 12:7-9).

The long shaft of the abyss means the long shaft leading to the abyss. The abyss is the bottomless pit of Revelation 20:3. The abyss and Hades may be synonymous terms (Romans 10:7). Our Lord probably referred to this in

Matthew 12:40 in speaking of His own descent into the heart of the earth. The body of Jesus was not buried in the earth, certainly not in the heart of the earth, rather He went to the abyss to announce that His redemption had been wrought. It behooves us not to be dogmatic where Scripture is silent, but there is the thought that a shaft leads from the surface to the heart of the earth. Our Lord now holds the key (Revelation 1:18). Demons are imprisoned there (II Peter 2:4).

> And Jesus asked him, saying, What is thy name? And he said, Legion: because many devils were entered into him. And they besought him that he would not command them to go out into the deep [abyss] (Luke 8:30, 31).

During the last part of the Great Tribulation, this key is given to Satan. That perhaps explains why men cannot die during this period. Satan wants to keep them alive.

Verse 2—And he opened the bottomless pit; and there arose a smoke out of the pit, as the smoke of a great furnace; and the sun and the air were darkened by reason of the smoke of the pit.

And he opened the long shaft (pit, well) of the abyss, and there came smoke out of the long shaft of the abyss as the smoke of a great furnace; and the sun and the air were darkened from the smoke of the shaft of the abyss.

Out of the shaft, like a great erupting volcano, will come smoke to cover the entire earth. This is smog of the most vicious type. The literal interpretation of this verse is the correct and most satisfying one.

Verses 3, 4—And there came out of the smoke locusts upon the earth; and unto them was given power, as the scorpions of the earth have power. And it was commanded them that they should not hurt the grass of the earth, neither any green thing, neither any tree; but only those men which have not the seal of God in their foreheads.

And out of the smoke came forth locusts upon the earth, and power was given to them as the scorpions of the earth have power. And it was said to them in order that they should not hurt the grass of the earth nor any green things, nor any tree, but only (except) the men who do not have the seal of God on their foreheads.

These are locusts but of a different character. As Govet remarks, they are "no common locusts:

(1) for they eat no vegetable productions;

(2) the locusts of the earth have no king (Proverbs 30:27), these have;

(3) in the plague of Egypt the inspired recorder had said, "Before them there were no such locusts as they, neither after them shall be such' (Exodus 10:14);

(4) yet they are literal creatures, resembling the literal animals named: the lion, the horse, the scorpion, the man."

This is a plague of locusts which is as literal as the plague of locusts in Egypt (see Exodus 10:14, 15). Joel prophesied of a coming plague of locusts (see Joel 1). The difference is the character of the locusts and the object of their destruction. They sting as scorpions and their objects are evil men.

Verse 5—And to them it was given that they should not kill them, but that they should be tormented five months: and their torment was as the torment of a scorpion, when he striketh a man.

And it was given to them in order that they should not kill them, but in order that they should be tormented five months; and their torment was as the torment of a scorpion, when it striketh a man.

The scorpion is shaped as a lobster, and lives in damp places. His sting is in his tail; though not fatal, it is very painful.

Verse 6—And in those days shall men seek death, and shall not find it; and shall desire to die, and death shall flee from them.

And in those days shall the men seek death, and shall not find it; and they shall earnestly desire to die, and death fleeth from them.

This refers to the men—the evil men. The severe punishment does not produce repentance, but a desire to die. There would be wholesale suicide, were it not prevented. Why are they unable to commit suicide? Is it because Satan has the key of the shaft of the bottomless pit, and will not let his followers leave the earth scene where the battle of Light and Darkness is being waged? Or is God making these men face up to the music from which there is no escape? It would appear that the former explanation is more acceptable.

Verses 7-10—And the shapes of the locusts were like unto horses prepared unto battle; and on their heads were as it were crowns like gold, and their faces were as the faces of men. And they had hair as the hair of women, and their teeth were as the teeth of lions. And they had breastplates, as it were breastplates of iron; and the sound of their wings was as the sound of chariots of many horses running to battle. And they had tails like unto scorpions, and there were stings in their tails: and their power was to hurt men five months.

And the likenesses of the locusts were like unto horses prepared for war; and on their heads were as it were crowns like gold, and their faces were as the faces of men. And they had hair as the hair of women, and their teeth were as the teeth of lions. And they had breastplates, as it were breastplates of iron; and the sound of their wings was as of chariots of many horses rushing into battle. And they had tails like scorpions, and stings; and in their tails was their power to hurt men five months.

This is a detailed description of the locusts. It is frightful, weird, and unnatural at first inspection. However, a closer examination of the text, reveals a striking similarity to the locusts of Palestine. Dr. Vincent comments, "The likeness of a locust to a horse, especially to a horse equipped with armor, is so striking that the insect is named in German *Heupferd hay-horse*, and in Italian *cavaletta little horse.*"

Also, the faces of locusts resemble the faces of men. The antennae of the locust is compared to a girl's hair. Joel compares the teeth of the locust with those of a lion (Joel 1:6). Many have commented on the weird sound that locusts make. Vincent quotes Olivier, a French writer: "It is difficult to express the effect produced on us by the sight of the whole atmosphere filled on all sides and to a great height by an innumerable quantity of these insects, whose flight was slow and uniform, and whose noise resembled that of rain."

It would appear that the natural characteristics of the locust are carried over and magnified in these unnatural locusts. It is repeated again, these locusts hurt man for five months. The opening of the abyss by Satan releases these unnatural creatures, which are probably demon possessed, yet are restricted in their activity. They are restrained from harming the world of nature which received the impact of the first four trumpets. God now closes in on man in judgment.

Verse 11—And they had a king over them, which is the angel of the bottomless pit, whose name in the Hebrew tongue is Abaddon, but in the Greek tongue hath his name Apollyon.

They have over them (as) king, the angel of the abyss: his name in Hebrew is Abaddon, and in the Greek tongue he hath the name Apollyon.

These locusts are further differentiated from ordinary locusts, as *they have a king over them,* "the locusts have no king" (Proverbs 30:27). This leader is one of the fallen angels, the chief henchman of Satan. He is permitted to lead an invasion of earth for the first time (see Revelation 11:7).

Abaddon means destruction,

Apollyon means destroyer.

Verse 12—One woe is past; and, behold, there come two woes more hereafter.

The one woe is past; behold there come yet two woes after these things.

The first woe introduced the last half of the Great Tribulation period and it had a duration of five months. Apparently the last two woes cover the remainder of the period, and the warning here indicates that worse things are to follow. The next trumpet reveals it to be no idle warning.

g. SIXTH Trumpet—Angels Loosed at River Euphrates, verses 13-21

Verses 13, 14—And the sixth angel sounded, and I heard a voice from the four horns of the golden altar which is before God, saying to the sixth angel which had the trumpet, Loose the four angels which are bound in the great river Euphrates.

And the sixth angel blew the trumpet (sounded). And I heard one (a single) voice out of the horns of the golden altar which is before God, saying to the sixth angel having the trumpet, loose the four angels which have been bound at the great river Euphrates.

When the sixth angel blew the trumpet, a command came from the horns of the golden altar. This is where the angel offered prayer at the beginning of the blowing of the trumpets (8:3). The sixth angel not only blows the trumpet but is given a command to loose four angels bound at the river Euphrates. This angel received, in turn, his orders from Christ, who has now ripped off the seven seals from the title deed of this earth.

The angels who are bound are evidently evil, for why were they bound? Releasing them turns loose a flood tide of destruction on the earth. They were bound, away from the others, because of the enormity of their crime.

Why were they bound at this particular location? Though this may be difficult to explain, the prominence of this area in Scripture cannot be overlooked. The Garden of Eden was somewhere in this section; sin of mankind began here; the first murder was committed here; the first war was fought here; here was the flood and the Tower of Babel; to this area were brought the Israelites of the Babylonian Captivity; Babylon was the fountainhead of idolatry; and here is the final surge of sin.

The Euphrates marks the division between East and West. Kipling said that east is east and west is west and never the twain shall meet. Perhaps there has been a restraining influence in the past which has kept the hordes from the East from spilling over into the West, but it will be broken down (see Revelation 16:12). From the time of Alexander the Great the white man has had his day. Colonialism as far as the white man is concerned is over, but Communism's colonialism is on the march. The dark races are awakening. They have been held back, and apparently these four angels had something to do with holding them back.

Zechariah locates Babylon as the last stand of false religion (Zechariah 5).

Verses 15, 16—And the four angels were loosed, which were prepared for an hour, and a day, and a month, and a year, for to slay the third part of men. And the number of the army of the horsemen were two hundred thousand thousand: and I heard the number of them.

And the four angels were loosed, who had been prepared for the hour, and day, and month, and year, that they might kill the third of men. And the number of the armies of the cavalry was two ten thousands (myriads) of ten thousands (myriads).

The period of time is not indicated here, as is evident by the omission of the article and the preposition with *day, and month and year*. The exact moment that they are to be released is emphasized—the *hour* which shall fall on the appointed *day, month* and year. The time is accurately determined when will begin this invasion of what Dr. Newell labels, "hellish horsemen." It is the zero hour.

The size of the army is stupendous. It is numbered at 200 million. These are not human beings. It is wholesale invasion of the demon world, which is a further result of Satan opening the door of the shaft of the bottomless pit. The following description of these horsemen further confirms this fact.

Verses 17, 18—And thus I saw the horses in the vision, and them that sat on them, having breastplates of fire, and of jacinth, and brimstone: and the heads of the horses were as the heads of lions; and out of their mouths issued fire and smoke and brimstone. By these three was the third part of men killed, by the fire, and by the smoke, and by the brimstone, which issued out of their mouths.

And, thus (after this manner) I saw the horses in the (my) vision, and those that sat on them, have breastplates as of fire (fiery red), and hyacinth, and brimstone; and the heads of the horses were as the heads of lions; and out of their mouths proceed fire, and smoke, and brimstone. By these three plagues was the third of men killed, by the fire, and the smoke, and the brimstone that proceeded out of their mouths.

The colors are as striking as the horsemen are unnatural:

Fire is *fiery red.*

Hyacinth is the same color as the flower—dull, dark blue.

Brimstone is light yellow.

77

The *horse* is the animal of war (Job 39:19-25). Hell is now making war on mankind.

These creatures are unnatural and are probably demons or demon controlled. This is a literal description of them. Newell makes this timely comment, "Believe, and you scarcely need any comment." These three plagues are literal. The fire is literal; the smoke is literal; the brimstone is literal. (See Genesis 19).

One third of the population of earth is killed. Previously one third of nature had been affected (see chapter 8), but mankind had not been touched. If the population of the world was 1½ billion, then this would mean that 500,000,000 would be slain. It must be remembered that a fourth part of mankind had been slain under the fourth seal (6:8). This terrible decimation of the earth's population seemed incongruous with all of history until an atomic bomb fell upon Hiroshima. Since then, men have been using more frightening language than that of Revelation. They now talk of the total decimation of earth's inhabitants.

One final word concerning these hellish horsemen must suffice. The horsemen do not do the killing. They have only defensive weapons. The horses do the slaying. This is not the jet plane, to be sure, but the analogy is here and should be noted.

Verse 19—For their power is in their mouth, and in their tails: for their tails were like unto serpents, and had heads, and with them they do hurt.

For the power of the horses is in their mouths, and in their tails; for their tails were like serpents, having heads, and by them they hurt.

These unnatural horses are able to kill with their mouths. The weirdest feat of all is that, instead of horses' hair for a tail, they have serpents which also are used in destroying mankind. They kill with the mouth, and they hurt with the tail.

Verses 20, 21—And the rest of the men which were not killed by these plagues yet repented not of the works of their hands, that they should not worship devils, and idols of gold, and silver, and brass, and stone, and of wood: which neither can see, nor hear, nor walk: neither repented they of their murders, nor of their sorceries, nor of their fornication, nor of their thefts.

And the rest of men who were not killed by these plagues, repented not of the works of their hands, that they should not worship demons, and idols of gold and silver and copper and stone and wood, which can neither see, nor hear, nor walk. Neither repented they of their murders, nor of their sorceries, nor of their fornication, nor of their thefts.

What is the reaction of mankind who was not killed by the judgments of the trumpets? Surely such severe judgments will cause them to repent and turn to God for salvation. Nothing of the kind transpires. This seems strange, but it is not unique. In our day there was no turning to God during the Dust Bowl and depression, and the fear occasioned by the atomic bomb is disappearing and Americans continue to live as though there were no God. Likewise during the Tribulation they continue in the worship of demons and idols. There is a strange alliance between demonism and idolatry. Satan is back of all idolatry and false religion. Demonism will spread like a deadly virus through the earth during the Great Tribulation. The activity of the 144,000 witnesses for God will cause Satan to become extremely active in the same period.

They not only fail to desist from false worship, but they continue in a life of active sin. They do not repent of murder. Capital punishment will probably be suspended in this period and God's mandate against murder, as well as idolatry, will be ignored.

Sorceries is in the Greek *pharmakeion,* from which we get our word pharmacy. It is the Greek word for drugs, and means the use of drugs in influencing others for evil purposes. Evidently drug addiction in this period will be prevalent. It will be one of the means employed by Antichrist to make the population subservient to his will. A statement from Seiss is pertinent here.

> We have only to think of the use of alcoholic stimulants, of opium, of tobacco, of the rage of cosmetics and medicaments to increase love attractions, of resorts to the pharmacopoeia in connection with sensuality—of the magical agents and treatments alleged to come from the spirit-world for the benefit of people in this—of the thousand impositions in the way of medicines and remedial agents, encouraging mankind to reckless transgression with the hope of easily repairing the damages of nature's penalties—of the growing prevalence of crime induced by these things, setting loose and stimulating to activity the vilest passions, which are eating out the moral sense of society—for the beginnings of that moral degeneracy to which the seer here alludes as characteristic of the period when the sixth trumpet is sounded.

Fornication indicates that the emphasis in the Great Tribulation is still upon sex. Adultery will abound.

Robbery will likewise be prevalent. It is a time of lawlessness when all of God's commandments will be repudiated. The shortage of foodstuffs, brought about by universal destruction in nature, will cause men to murder and steal to satisfy their needs and those of their families. The severe pressures and punishment of the Great Tribulation will not change the hard and impenitent hearts of men. They continue to believe the devil's lie. See II Thessalonians 2:9-12.

> Even him, whose coming is after the working of Satan with all power and signs and lying wonders, and with all deceivableness of unrighteousness in them that perish; because they received not the love of the truth, that they might be saved. And for this cause God shall send them strong delusion, that they should believe a lie: that they all might be damned who believe not the truth, but had pleasure in unrighteousness (II Thessalonians 2:9-12).

Chapter 10

THEME: The Mighty Angel with a Little Book descends from heaven. He gives John the Little Book, and he eats it.

OUTLINE:

h. **INTERLUDE** Between the Sixth and Seventh Trumpets, 10:1-11:14

   (1) The Strong Angel with the Little Book, verses 1-7

   (2) John Eats the Little Book, verses 8-11

REMARKS:

This chapter begins the second in a series of interludes between the 6th and 7th objects used to describe the various phases of the Great Tribulation. Between the 6th and 7th seals there were two groups who were redeemed during the Great Tribulation. Here, between the 6th and 7th trumpets, we have three personalities introduced. In this chapter the mighty angel is described. In chapter 11 the two witnesses are introduced—though not identified.

There has been definite disagreement as to the identity of the mighty angel. Many outstanding expositors (Godet, Vincent, Pettingill, DeHaan, and Ironside) identify him as Christ. Newell and others consider him to be an angel of great power and authority, but not Christ. There is ample evidence to show that he is only a mighty angel. Christ does not appear in Revelation as an angel. It is true that in the Old Testament the pre-incarnate Christ was seen as the Angel of the Lord, but after He took on our humanity we do not see Him as an angel. Here He is revealed as the post-incarnate Christ, who is glorified and exalted to the "nth" degree. It is well to keep before us constantly that this book is the unveiling of Jesus Christ. New glories of His person, power, and performance are unfolded in each chapter.

COMMENT:

   (1) The Strong Angel with the Little Book, verses 1-7

Verse 1—And I saw another mighty angel come down from heaven, clothed with a cloud: and a rainbow was upon his head, and his face was as it were the sun, and his feet as pillars of fire:

And I saw another strong (powerful) angel coming down out of heaven clothed with a cloud, and the rainbow was upon his head, and his face was as the sun, and his feet as pillars of fire.

Another strong angel seems to make it clear that this is not Christ. The first strong angel, introduced in 5:2 clearly is not Christ. It is the livery of this angel that has led some to identify him as Christ. Though all angels are the servants of Christ, in this final book of the Bible, this is evidently the special envoy of Christ, bearing all the credentials of his exalted position. He comes down out of heaven from the presence of Christ, who is in the midst of the throne.

Clothed with a cloud is his uniform, as a special envoy from Christ. Although the clouds of glory are associated with the Second Coming of Christ, the angel described here is not coming in clouds of glory, but is clothed with a cloud. Furthermore, this is not the Second Coming of Christ; rather, this angel makes the announcemnt that He is coming soon. Angels, you recall, announced His First Coming.

Rainbow upon his head is the cap for his uniform. This is a reminder of God's covenant with man (see Revelation 4:3).

His face was as the sun is his badge of identification. This is the signature of the glorified Christ (see Revelation 1:16). It does not follow that this one must be, therefore, the Son of God, for Moses' face shone after he had been in the presence of God (Exodus 34:29). The raiment of the creatures at the resurrection of Christ also shone (Luke 24:4). The angel of Revelation 18:1 is a light giver, as the sun and moon, yet no one asserts that he is Christ.

His feet as pillars of fire is still part of the uniform of Christ's special envoy (see Revelation 1:15). He has come to make a special and solemn announcement of coming judgment. All of these features of identification are his credentials and connect him to the Person of Christ as His special envoy.

Verses 2, 3—And he had in his hand a little book open: and he set his right foot upon the sea, and his left foot on the earth, and cried with a loud voice, as when a lion roareth: and when he had cried, seven thunders uttered their voices.

And he had in his hand a little book opened; and he set his right foot upon the sea, and his left foot upon the earth; and he cried with a great voice as (when) a lion roareth: and when he cried the seven thunders spoke their own voices.

This little book appears to be the same book as was originally in the hands of the Father (Revelation 5:1). It should be noted how it is first transferred to the nail-pierced hands of God the Son, who in turn transfers it to the angel who gives it, finally, to John to eat. This is the book of the title deed of the earth. It contains the judgments of the Great Tribulation, by which the Lord Jesus is coming to power. The book is now opened and the judgments are on display. This book is his authority for claiming both the sea and the earth for Christ—God claims the land:

> The land shall not be sold for ever: for the land is mine; for ye are strangers and sojourners with me (Leviticus 25:23).

God claims the sea and the land:

> Thou madest him to have dominion over the works of thy hands; thou hast put all things under his feet: all sheep and oxen, yea, and the beasts of the field; the fowl of the air, and the fish of the sea, and whatsoever passeth through the paths of the seas (Psalm 8: 6-8).

Those who have discovered different areas of the Western Hemisphere, beginning with Columbus, claimed it in the name of their king and country by planting the flag upon the shore.

With the title deed of this earth in his hand, and by placing his right foot on the sea and his left foot upon the earth, in a great voice he claims all for Christ. The kingdoms of this world will become the kingdoms of the Lord Jesus Christ through judgment. As creator and redeemer, the world belongs to Him.

The book is described here as a *little book* because the time of the Great Tribulation is short:

For he will finish the work, and cut it short in righteousness: because a short work will the Lord make upon the earth (Romans 9:28).

The seven thunders is God's amen to the angel's claim—"the God of glory thundereth" (Psalm 29:3).

God thundereth marvellously with his voice; great things doeth he, which we cannot comprehend (Job 37:5).

Vincent makes this comment, "The Jews were accustomed to speak of thunder as 'the seven voices.'" See Psalm 29 where "the voice of the Lord" occurs seven times.

Verse 4—And when the seven thunders had uttered their voices, I was about to write: and I heard a voice from heaven saying unto me, Seal up those things which the seven thunders uttered, and write them not.

And when the seven thunders spoke, I was about to write; and I heard a voice from heaven saying, Seal up the things which the seven thunders spoke and write them not.

John was a scribe taking down the visions as they were given to him (Revelation 1:11). He was about to write what the seven thunders had spoken, but was forbidden to do so.

This is the only place in the book of Revelation where anything is sealed (Revelation 22:10). If this angel were Christ, then John probably would have fallen down and worshipped Him (Revelation 1:17).

Is is mere assumption to presume to know what the thunders spoke. Wild speculators have made ridiculous guesses. Vitringa interpreted them as the seven crusades; Danbuz made them the seven nations that received the reformation; Elliott makes them the pope's bull against Luther; and Seventh-day Adventism has presumed to reveal the things which were uttered.

Christ said to seal them up by not writing them down. They remain to this day, a secret. (Evidently He considered that which John had written to be clear and not sealed—though there are men who say that the entire book of Revelation is "sealed.")

Verses 5, 6—And the angel which I saw stand upon the sea and upon the earth lifted up his hand to heaven, and sware by him that liveth for ever and ever, who created heaven, and the things that therein are, and the earth, and the things that therein are, and the sea, and the things which are therein, that there should be time no longer.

And the angel whom I saw standing upon the sea and upon the earth lifted up his right hand to heaven, and sware by (in) Him that liveth for ever and ever (into the ages of the ages), who created heaven and the things in it, and the sea and the things in it, that there shall be no longer delay.

This angel could not be Christ, since he takes an oath by the Eternal Creator, *by Him that liveth for ever and ever.* If he were Christ, he would sware by Himself:

For when God made promise to Abraham, because he could swear by no greater, he sware by himself (Hebrews 6:13).

This angel swore by another, not by himself.

The Lord Jesus Christ is the Eternal God:

> In the beginning was the Word, and the Word was with God, and the Word was God. The same was in the beginning with God (John 1:1, 2).

The Lord Jesus himself made this declaration:

> Jesus said unto them, Verily, verily, I say unto you, Before Abraham was, I am (John 8:58).

Christ is the Creator:

> All things were made by him; and without him was not any thing made that was made (John 1:3).

> For by him were all things created, that are in heaven, and that are in earth, visible and invisible, whether they be thrones, or dominions, or principalities, or powers: all things were created by him, and for him (Colossians 1:16).

The angel takes an oath in the name of Christ who is in heaven. As Christ's representative he claims it all for Christ.

Time will not run out, time will not cease, *there should be time no longer* actually means *there shall be no longer delay*. It is the glad announcement from heaven to God's saints on earth, meaning that the time now is very brief before Christ returns. It is a confirmation of the words of Christ in His Olivet Discourse:

> And except those days should be shortened, there should no flesh be saved but for the elect's sake those days shall be shortened (Matthew 24:22).

Evidently the first part of the Great Tribulation—until the blowing of the sixth trumpet—caused God's servants on earth to wonder how much longer they must endure, "but he that shall endure unto the end, the same shall be saved" (Matthew 24:13).

It is likewise in answer to the prayers of the martyrs (Revelation 6:10). It is good news for God's saints. "The kingdom of heaven is at hand" is the substance of the angel's announcement. The long awaited kingdom, foreseen by the Old Testament prophets, has finally arrived. In these days of grace, swearing is forbidden (James 5:12), but under the Old Testament economy it was permitted. This is another indication that during the Tribulation there is a return to the economy of the Old Testament. They are no longer in the period of the Church's presence on earth.

Verse 7—But in the days of the voice of the seventh angel, when he shall begin to sound, the mystery of God should be finished, as he hath declared to his servants the prophets.

But in the days of the sound of the seventh angel, when he is about to blow (sound) (the trumpet), and the mystery of God is finished, as He gave the glad tidings to his servants, the prophets.

This all takes place when the seventh angel is preparing to blow the trumpet, which would seem to indicate that the seventh trumpet brings us to the conclusion of the Great Tribulation (see Revelation 11:15). It is at this time that the mystery of God is finally made clear. Many single facets of this mystery have been given as the total answer, yet it seems that this is greater than any one and is the sum total of all.

There is a mystery concerning the nation Israel, judgment, suffering, injustice, the silence of God, and the coming kingdom. The basic problem is, "Why did God permit evil and why has He tolerated it for so long a time?" At this point God will make it clear to all of His servants that He was wise, holy, just, and loving in permitting evil to enter His universe. All the problems and questions regarding sin and the suffering and pain in our own lives will be thoroughly explained to the entire satisfaction of all.

The glad tidings is the Gospel of the Kingdom, which is briefly, "the kingdom of heaven is at hand." This is the kingdom foretold by the prophets.

(2) John Eats the Little Book, verses 8-11

Verse 8—And the voice which I heard from heaven spake unto me again, and said, Go and take the little book which is open in the hand of the angel which standeth upon the sea and upon the earth.

And the voice which I heard out of heaven, (I heard) it again speaking with me, and saying, Go, take the book which is open in the hand of the angel who standeth upon the sea and upon the earth. .

The order comes from Christ in heaven, as He is directing every operation recorded in the book of Revelation. If the voice is not Christ's, then He has given the order to the angel to speak from heaven.

John has apparently returned to the earth in the Spirit. The Little Book that was formerly in the hand of God the Father is now transferred to John.

Verses 9, 10—And I went unto the angel, and said unto him, Give me the little book. And he said unto me, Take it, and eat it up; and it shall make thy belly bitter, but it shall be in thy mouth sweet as honey. And I took the little book out of the angel's hand, and ate it up; and it was in my mouth sweet as honey: and as soon as I had eaten it, my belly was bitter.

And I went away to the angel, saying to him, Give to me the little book, and he said to me, Take, and eat it up; and it shall make thy belly bitter, but in thy mouth it shall be as sweet as honey. And I took the little book out of the hand of the angel, and ate it up. And it was in my mouth as sweet as honey. And when I had eaten it, my belly was made bitter.

John becomes a participant in the great drama which he is recording. He is required to do a very strange thing—one that has typical meaning. He eats the Little Book, with bitter-sweet results. Eating the Little Book means to receive the Word of God with faith. Such is the teaching of the Word of God:

Thy words were found, and I did eat them; and thy word was unto me the joy and rejoicing of mine heart: for I am called by thy name, O LORD God of hosts (Jeremiah 15:16).

Moreover he said unto me, Son of man, eat that thou findest; eat this roll, and go speak unto the house of Israel. So I opened my mouth, and he caused me to eat that roll. And he said unto me, Son of man, cause thy belly to eat, and fill thy bowels with this roll that I give thee. Then did I eat it; and it was in my mouth as honey for sweetness (Ezekiel 3:1-3).

Pleasant words are as an honeycomb, sweet to the soul, and health to the bones (Proverbs 16:24).

How sweet are thy words unto my taste! yea, sweeter than honey to my mouth! (Psalm 119:103).

The part of the Word of God, taken by John, was judgment, which became bitter as he digested it, and speaks of sorrow and anguish because of judgment. (Compare Ruth 1:20, Ezekiel 2:9, 10 and 3:14.) John eagerly received the Word of God, but when he saw that more judgment was to follow, it brought travail of soul, and sorrow of heart—sweet in his mouth, bitter in his digestive system.

Many folk begin the study of prophecy with enthusiasm, but when they find that it is applicable to the life, and makes demands upon them personally, they lose interest and it becomes a bitter thing. "I can't eat that, it disagrees with me"—sweet to the taste, but causes spiritual indigestion.

Verse 11—And he said unto me, Thou must prophesy again before many peoples, and nations, and tongues, and kings.

And they say to me, It is necessary for you to prophecy again against peoples and nations and tongues and kings.

This is the reason that the Little Book became bitter to John. He must prophesy against many before Christ comes to His kingdom. Much prophecy is to follow. We are not quite one-half way through this book.

Prophecy *about* the nations and peoples is necessarily *against* them. The new series of prophecy, that is to begin, proves this. Beginning with chapter 12, the new series is the evidence.

The study of prophecy should have a definite effect upon the life of the believer.

Chapter 11

THEME: 42 months remaining of the Times of the Gentiles; the 2 witnesses to prophesy 42 months; the second Woe; the seventh Trumpet.

OUTLINE:

(3) **Date** for the Ending of "the Times of the Gentiles," verses 1, 2

(4) **Duration** of the Prophesying of the Two Witnesses, verses 3-12

(5) **Doom** of the Second Woe—Great Earthquake, verses 13, 14

i. **SEVENTH** Trumpet—End of Great Tribulation and Opening of Temple in Heaven, verses 15-19

REMARKS:

This chapter brings us to Old Testament ground. The temple, time periods, and the distinction between Jews and Gentiles indicate that we are again under the Old Testament economy.

Also we note the conclusion of the interlude between the 6th and 7th Trumpets and the blowing of the 7th Trumpet. It is also interesting to note that this chapter opens with the temple on earth and closes with the temple in heaven. The temple on earth is the temple of the Tribulation. The temple in heaven is the original from which Moses received the blueprint to make a tabernacle in the wilderness (see Exodus 25:40; Hebrews 8:2-5; 9:23, 24).

Chronologically the 7th Trumpet brings us to the Return of Christ at the end of the Great Tribulation. The Return of Christ is presented in detail in chapter 19. There it is the open heaven; here it is the open temple. Between chapters 11 and 19 many details of the Great Tribulation are filled in which would be otherwise unknown. Great personalities and nations that play a large part in this period have not previously come before us, but will be given in much detail beginning with chapter 12. The Jewish nation and the last half of the Great Tribulation are emphasized in this section. The interlude of this chapter introduces us to the prominence of Israel in this final period of 42 months or 3½ years (of Daniel's 70th Week of 7 years).

The temple in Jerusalem had been destroyed when John wrote this. He makes it clear that another temple will be built—which temple is a total rejection of Jesus Christ, for it repudiates all that He did on the cross. The temples of the Old Testament all pointed to Christ. This temple rejects Him, and will finally culminate in the worship of an image of Antichrist or the state over which he rules.

COMMENT:

(3) **Date** for the Ending of "the Times of the Gentiles," verses 1, 2

Verses 1, 2—And there was given me a reed like unto a rod: and the angel stood, saying, Rise, and measure the temple of God, and the altar, and them that worship therein. But the court which is without the temple leave out, and measure it not; for it is given unto the Gentiles: and the holy city shall they tread under foot forty and two months.

And there was given me a reed like a rod, saying, Rise and measure the temple (holy place) of God, and the altar, and them that worship therein. And the court which is without the temple cast out (ekbale—throw out) and measure it not; for it is given to the nations, and the holy city shall they tread under foot forty and two months.

A reed like a rod denotes the character of the unit of measurement. The rod is for chastisement and judgment:

> Thou shalt break them with a rod of iron; thou shalt dash them in pieces like a potter's vessel (Psalm 2:9).

The rod is for comfort:

> Yea, though I walk through the valley of the shadow of death, I will fear no evil: for thou art with me; thy rod and thy staff they comfort me (Psalm 23:4).

Both judgment and solace are in this chapter.

Rise and measure indicates that God is beginning to deal with the nation Israel again. (See Zechariah 2:1-4; 10-11; Jeremiah 31:38, 39.)

The temple of God is limited to the Holy Place and Holy of Holies. The temple of God places us back on Old Testament ground, for there is no temple given to the Church. The Church is a temple of the Holy Spirit:

> In whom all the building fitly framed together groweth unto an holy temple in the Lord: in whom ye also are builded together for an habitation of God through the Spirit (Ephesians 2:21, 22).

The altar refers to the golden altar of prayer (incense), since the altar of burnt offering was not in the temple proper.

Even the worshipers were to be measured. God does count the number of those who worship Him.

The court which is without the temple throw out (of the measuring) excludes all that does not belong to the temple proper (Holy Place and Holy of Holies). The altar of burnt offering would be on the outside. Since this altar was a picture of the cross of Christ, it would seem to mean that the gospel of the cross of Christ will still be available to all 'mankind during the intensity of this brief crisis.

It is given to the nations (Gentiles) declares that though this period still belongs to the Gentiles, their dominion is limited to 42 months. This confirms the word of our Lord:

> And they shall fall by the edge of the sword, and shall be led away captive into all nations: and Jerusalem shall be trodden down of the Gentiles, until the times of the Gentiles be fulfilled (Luke 21:24).

Forty and two months is the period identified with the last half of the Great Tribulation period—repeated again in Revelation 13:5. It is also given as 1260 days as in verse 3 of this chapter, and in Revelation 12:6. Also other terms are used as, "a time, times [dual], and half a time" or $3\frac{1}{2}$ years, Revelation 12:14. Daniel adopts this unit of measurement for this period (Daniel 7:25; 12:7). All of these evidently cover the same period of time which is the last half of Daniel's 70th Week (the 7-year Tribulation period). The Great Tribulation is divided into two equal periods (see Daniel 9:27; 12:10, 11; Matthew 24:15-21). While the first part is global and general, in the last period Israel becomes prominent.

These two verses indicate that God is beginning to deal again with Israel nationally, and that the time of the Gentiles is running out. God is making good the oath of the mighty angel who stated, "There shall be no longer delay."

(4) **Duration** of the Prophesying of the Two Witnesses, verses 3-12

Verse 3—And I will give power unto my two witnesses, and they shall prophesy a thousand two hundred and threescore days, clothed in sackcloth.

And I will give to my two witnesses, and they shall prophesy a thousand, two hundred and three score [60] days, clothed in sackcloth.

There is much difference of opinion as to the identity of the two witnesses. They are introduced without any suggestion as to who they are. Godet writes, "They are one of the most startling features of the book." If their identity was essential for the understanding of the book, there would have been some indication given about their persons.

As a result of the lack of information concerning them, there has been much speculation. Those who have espoused the historical view of the Revelation, have named them as John Huss, Pope Sylvester, Waldenson, and the Two Testaments. Those who hold the futurist view have not been in complete agreement. Seiss and Govett say they are Enoch and Elijah. The *Gospel of Nicodemus* contains the following, "I am Enoch who pleased God, and was translated by him. And this is Elijah the Tishbite. We are also to live to the end of the age: but then we are about to be sent by God to resist Antichrist, and be slain by him, and to rise after three days, and to be caught up in the clouds to meet the Lord." Dean Alford, Walter Scott, and Donald Barnhouse state they are Moses and Elijah. William Newell does not identify them. They could be two unknown witnesses.

That they are two *human* witnesses seems certain from the description given of them. Two is the required number of witnesses according to the law (Deuteronomy 17:6) and the Church (Matthew 18:16).

It seems almost certain that Elijah is one of them. It was predicted that he would return:

> Behold, I will send you Elijah the prophet before the coming of the great and dreadful day of the LORD (Malachi 4:5).

> And Jesus answered and said unto them, Elias truly shall first come, and restore all things (Matthew 17:11).

It is said in Revelation 11:4 that these two witnesses are "two lampstands *standing before the God* of the earth." A favorite expression of Elijah was, "As the LORD God of Israel liveth, *before whom I stand* . . ." (I Kings 17:1). The presence of Elijah on the Mount of Transfiguration further suggests this —but would necessitate the second witness being Moses, which is more difficult to sustain.

We suggest that John the Baptist is the second witness. He was the forerunner of Christ at His first coming. He was similar to Elijah in manner and message. Both knew what it was to oppose the forces of darkness and stand alone for God against impossible odds. John the Baptist would be the witness of the New Testament, as Elijah would be for the Old Testament. John the Baptist was not part of the Church, the Bride of Christ, but was a "friend of the bridegroom."

It seems unlikely that Enoch would be one of the witnesses, since he was a Gentile. The fact that he did not die does not qualify him for the office, as by this time many in the Church will have been translated without dying.

A thousand two hundred and threescore days. The significant feature about the two witnesses is not their identity but the time they appear. Is it during the first half or the last half of the Great Tribulation period? The first half seems to fit the text more accurately. They testify until the Beast appears and then they are martyred (verse 7).

Clothed in sackcloth is the garb better suited to the period of Law than of Grace. It is becoming to both Elijah and John the Baptist (Jeremiah 4:8; Matthew 3:4).

Verses 4, 5—These are the two olive trees, and the two candlesticks standing before the God of the earth. And if any man will hurt them, fire proceedeth out of their mouth, and devoureth their enemies; and if anyone wishes to hurt them, thus must he be killed.

These are the two olive trees and the two lampstands standing before the Lord of the earth. And if any one wishes to hurt them, fire proceedeth out of their mouth and devoureth their enemies; and if anyone wishes to hurt them, thus must he be killed.

The two olive trees immediately suggest the vision in Zechariah 4. There the lampstands are two individuals (Joshua and Zerubbabel). They are enabled by the Holy Spirit to stand against insurmountable difficulties. The explanation is found in the words, "Not by might, nor by power, but by my Spirit saith the Lord of hosts" (Zechariah 4:6). The Holy Spirit will be present during the Great Tribulation. These two witnesses are lights before the powers of darkness. These men are accorded miraculous power to bring fire down from heaven—they are filled with the Holy Spirit. Here again, the suggestion is strongly in favor of Elijah (see I Kings 18:38 and II Kings 1:10). Also John made an announcement about one baptizing with fire (see Matthew 3:11). These two witnesses are immortal and immune to all attacks until their mission is completed. It is encouraging to know that all God's men are immortal until He is through with them.

Verse 6—These have power to shut heaven, that it rain not in the days of their prophecy: and have power over waters to turn them to blood, and to smite the earth with all plagues, as often as they will.

These have the authority [exousian—power] to shut up the heaven, that the rain may not wet during the days of their prophecy; and they have power over the waters to turn them into blood, and to smite the earth with every plague, as often as they wish.

These two witnesses are granted unlimited authority. They control rainfall on the earth. This again reminds us of Elijah (see I Kings 17:1; James 5:17). They can turn rivers, lakes and seas into blood. This reminds us of Moses (see Exodus 7:19).

Smite—they are given the same power Christ will have when He returns (see Revelation 19:15).

Every plague suggests the plagues Moses imposed on Egypt, but the plagues here are greater in number, as the territory is more vast.

As often as they wish reveals the confidence God places in these faithful servants.

Verse 7—And when they shall have finished their testimony, the beast that ascendeth out of the bottomless pit shall make war against them, and shall overcome them, and kill them.

And when they shall have finished their testimony, the wild beast that cometh up out of the abyss, shall make war with them, and overcome them, and kill them.

Finished their testimony reveals again that they are immortal until their work is accomplished. All of God's servants occupy this sure position.

The wild beast is the one yet to be introduced in Revelation 13:1. These two witnesses are slain by the Antichrist, as Jezebel attempted to slay Elijah, and as Herod slew John the Baptist.

And overcome them denotes that this is the temporary victory of darkness over light, evil over righteousness, hell over heaven, and Satan over God (see Revelation 13:4). These witnesses live up to their names—martyrs (the Greek word *martus*, translated *martyr*, is the word for *witness*).

Verse 8—And their dead bodies shall lie in the street of the great city, which spiritually is called Sodom and Egypt, where also our Lord was crucified.

And their dead bodies (carcasses) shall lie upon the street of the great city, which spiritually is called Sodom and Egypt, where also their Lord was crucified.

They are not even accorded a decent burial. This reveals the crude, cold barbarism of the last days—covered with but a thin veneer of culture. There is a strange resemblance to the sadistic curiosity which placed two dead men, Lenin and Stalin, on display in Red Square in Moscow. The word used for *bodies* denotes the contempt and hatred the world has for the two witnesses. They are treated as dead animals.

The great city is Jerusalem. It was likened unto Sodom by Isaiah (see Isaiah 1:10). It is called Egypt because the world has entered into every fibre of its life—social and political. It is conclusively identified as Jerusalem by the sad designation, *where also their Lord was crucified.*

Verse 9—And they of the people and kindreds and tongues and nations shall see their dead bodies three days and an half, and shall not suffer their dead bodies to be put in graves.

And out of the peoples, and tribes, and tongues, and nations do some gaze upon their dead bodies (carcasses) to be put in a tomb.

After Christ was crucified even Pilate permitted His friends to take down the body and give it a respectable burial (Mark 15:45). Not so with these two witnesses, for the world will be startled to hear that they are dead, and some will be skeptical. Apparently a television camera, or whatever is the latest gadget in that day, will play upon their features for three days and a half. The morbid curiosity of a godless society will relish the opportunity of gazing with awe upon their dead bodies. This is the worst indignity that a depraved world could vent upon the men who denounced them and their wicked ways.

Perhaps the witnesses had predicted their resurrection, and to prevent the possibility of another empty tomb, there was no burial and eyes were watching them every hour of the day and night.

Three days and a half reminds us that our Lord was in the tomb three days.

Verse 10—And they that dwell upon the earth shall rejoice over them, and make merry, and shall send gifts one to another; because these two prophets tormented them that dwelt on the earth.

And the dwellers upon the earth rejoice over them, and make merry, and shall send gifts one to another; because these two prophets tormented (vexed) the dwellers on the earth.

The death of the two witnesses is an occasion of high carnival on the earth. The world engages in a modern Christmas and Mardi Gras both rolled into one. The world has adopted the philosophy, "Let us eat, drink and be merry for tomorrow we die." Dr. Newell writes, "Now comes the real revelation of the heart of man: glee, horrid, insane, inhuman, hellish, ghoulish glee!"

And shall send gifts one to another indicates a very lovely occasion on the surface, but this is the devil's Christmas. The modern celebration of Christmas gets farther and farther from the birth of Christ and closer and closer to paganism. The day will come when it will be anti-Christian. Here it is the celebration of what Antichrist has done, rather than the celebration of the coming of Christ to Bethlemem.

Verse 11—And after three days and a half the Spirit of life from God entered into them, and they stood upon their feet; and great fear fell upon them which saw them.

And after the three days and a half the breath (spirit) of life from God entered into them, and they stood upon their feet; and great fear fell upon them that beheld them.

While the world is celebrating in jubilation the death of these witnesses and the television cameras are focused upon them, the witnesses will stand up on their feet. This is the Scriptural word for resurrection (histeme). They are of the Tribulation saints who have part in the first resurrection (see Revelation 20:4-6).

The news agency that has its television cameras turned on these two witnesses will have the "scoop" of the ages. If the death of the two witnesses was amazing, then their resurrection is shocking and terrifying. Though by this time men may be going to the moon, this will be something new for even that scientific age.

Verse 12—And they heard a great voice from heaven saying unto them, Come up hither. And they ascended up to heaven in a cloud; and their enemies beheld them.

And they heard a great voice out of heaven saying to them, Come up here, and they went up into heaven in the cloud, and their enemies beheld them.

The two witnesses heard *a great voice*, the voice of the archangel (I Thessalonians 4:16). Their enemies apparently did not hear the voice but they saw them go up into heaven. Again, the television camera would be ideal to record this—to be viewed by a terrified world. In contrast, Christ's enemies did not see Him ascend.

91

We have the *resurrection of the 2 witnesses in verse* 11,

We have the *ascension* of the 2 witnesses in verse 12.

The cloud of glory is associated with the ascension and coming of Christ.

(5) **Doom** of the Second Woe—Great Earthquake, verses 13, 14

Verse 13—And the same hour was there a great earthquake, and the tenth part of the city fell, and in the earthquake were slain of men seven thousand: and the remnant were afrighted, and gave glory to the God of heaven.

And in that hour there came to pass a great earthquake, and a tenth of the city fell, and 7000 names of men were killed in the earthquake, and the rest were afraid, and gave glory to the God of heaven.

It would appear that this earthquake is limited to the city of Jerusalem, as it was when Christ arose from the dead (see Matthew 28:2), and also at His crucifixion (See Matthew 27:51, 52).

One tenth of rebuilt Jerusalem falls. 7000 are slain. In reverse ratio 7000 was the number of the preserved remnant in Elijah's day. The earthquake, however, is for judgment.

Names of men is an idiom to indicate that they were men of prominence (Genesis 6:4), who had gone along with Antichrist; men whose names got into the headlines when Antichrist came to power.

Verse 14—The second woe is past; and, behold, the third woe cometh quickly.

This ends the 2nd Woe. The 3rd Woe begins shortly, though not immediately. The 3rd Woe is not the blowing of the 7th Trumpet, as that leads us beyond the Great Tribulation into the Millennium. The 7th Trumpet likewise opens up to us the 7 Personalities of chapters 12 and 13. The 3rd Woe begins when Satan is cast down to earth (see Revelation 12:12).

i. **SEVENTH** Trumpet—End of Great Tribulation and Opening of Temple in Heaven, verses 15-19

Verses 15-18—And the seventh angel sounded; and there were great voices in heaven, saying, The kingdoms of this world are become the kingdoms of our Lord, and of his Christ; and he shall reign for ever and ever. And the four and twenty elders, which sat before God on their seats, fell upon their faces, and worshipped God, saying, We give thee thanks, O Lord God Almighty, which art, and wast, and art to come; because thou hast taken to thee thy great power, and hast reigned. And the nations were angry, and thy wrath is come, and the time of the dead, that they should be judged, and that thou shouldest give reward unto thy servants the prophets, and to the saints, and them that fear thy name, small and great; and shouldest destroy them which destroy the earth.

And the seventh angel blew the trumpet; and there followed (came to pass) great voices in heaven, saying, The kingdom of the world (cosmos) is become (the kingdom) of our Lord, and of His Christ; and He shall reign unto the ages of the ages (for ever and ever). And the twenty-four elders, sitting before God on their thrones, fell upon their faces, and worshipped God, saying, We give thanks to you, O Lord God the Almighty, who art and who wast; because thou hast taken thy great power and didst reign. And the nations were angry (wroth), and thy wrath came, and the time (period) of the dead to be judged, and to give the reward to your servants the prophets and to the saints and to them that fear thy name, the small and great; and to destroy those who destroy (corrupt, the destroyers of) the earth.

The blowing of the 7th Trumpet is of utmost significance and is of special relevance in the understanding of the remainder of this book. In the program of God it brings us chronologically to the breath-taking entrance of eternity where the mystery of God is finally unraveled (see Revelation 10:7). It brings us in God's program as far as Revelation 21 where eternity begins. The broad outline of events which are significant to God is given to us here by the Holy Spirit. This section is a summary syllabus and synopsis of events up to the door of eternity. The following list will help focus these events in our minds:

(1) *Great voices in heaven* followed the blowing of the 7th Trumpet. After the opening of the 7th Seal, there was silence in heaven (Revelation 8:1). The contrast should be noted, because the blowing of the 7th Trumpet reveals God's program and clears up the mystery of God. All of God's created intelligences can see the end now and are jubilant in anticipation of the termination of evil being so close at hand.

(2) *The kingdom of the world (cosmos) is become (the kingdom) of our Lord and of His Christ, and He shall reign unto the ages of the ages (for ever and ever).*

It is not kingdoms (plural) but kingdom (singular) —denoting the fact that the kingdoms of this world are at present under Satan, to whom there is no distinction of nations, no East or West, no iron curtain, all are his, both sides are included in his domain. When Christ was here, Satan offered Him the kingdoms of the world. Our Lord called him "the prince of this world." This is the one-world that men are striving to bring into existence, the kingdom with which the United Nations is presently concerned. It is the totality of a civilization and society of which men boast of improvement, but which becomes more godless and wicked each day. It is a condemned civilization.

Of our Lord and of His Christ reminds us that the kingdom had to be subdued, for rebellion had broken out against the Lord and His Christ (Messiah, Anointed) at the arrest of Jesus.

> The kings of the earth set themselves, and the rulers take counsel together, against the LORD, and against his anointed, saying, Let us break their bands asunder, and cast away their cords from us (Psalm 2:2, 3).

This was recognized by the early church:

> And being let go, they went to their own company, and reported all that the chief priests and elders had said unto them. And when they heard that, they lifted up their voice to God with one accord, and said, Lord, thou art God, which hast made heaven, and earth, and the sea, and all that in them is: who by the mouth of thy servant David hast said, Why did the heathen rage, and the people imagine vain things? The kings of the earth stood up, and the rulers were gathered together against the Lord, and against his Christ (Acts 4:23-26).

Man's rebellion has been mounting up with a mighty crescendo from that day to this and will continue until Christ comes to put it down.

> Thou shalt break them with a rod of iron; thou shalt dash them in pieces like a potter's vessel (Psalm 2:9).

> And I saw heaven opened, and behold a white horse; and he that sat upon him was called Faithful and True, and in righteousness he doth judge and make war. His eyes were as a flame of fire, and on his head were many crowns; and he had a name written, that no man knew, but he himself. And he was clothed with a vesture dipped in blood: and his name is called The Word of God. And the armies which were in heaven followed him upon white horses, clothed in fine linen, white and clean. And out of his mouth goeth a sharp sword, that with it he should smite the nations: and he shall rule them with a rod of iron: and he treadeth the winepress of the fierceness and wrath of Almighty God. And he hath on his vesture and on his thigh a name written, KING OF KINGS, AND LORD OF LORDS (Revelation 19:11-16).

He shall reign unto the ages of the ages (for ever and ever) is the all inclusive term which encompasses the Millennial reign, the final rebellion, the Great White Throne and the eternal state. It begins with the Return of Christ—as we shall see in Revelation 19:11. The Millennial kingdom is but one phase of the eternal kingdom, it marks the beginning of the eternal kingdom. The end of the Millennial kingdom brings to an end God's testing of man, and introduces the final judgment, after which the kingdom continues on into eternity.

The 7th Trumpet brings us to the eternal kingdom, which is as far as we go chronologically in the book of the Revelation. (There will be much detail to fill in.)

Jericho is representative of the world. Jericho was compassed about for seven days and fell at the blowing of the trumpets:

> By faith the walls of Jericho fell down, after they were compassed about seven days (Hebrews 11:30).

The blowing of the seven trumpets and the blowing of the 7th Trumpet denotes the collapse of Satan's kingdom and the introduction of the reign of Christ. The 7th Trumpet also reveals the means whereby God will accomplish His purpose by introducing the 7 Personalities which figure prominently as actors in earth's last drama (chapters 12 and 13).

(3) *And the twenty-four elders, sitting before God, saying, we give thanks to you, O Lord God the Almighty, who art and who wast; because thou hast taken thy great power and didst reign.* This revelation causes the Church in heaven to worship and to celebrate the coming of Christ to the earth. This is a great victory celebration. The Church has prayed the prayer, "Thy kingdom come." Here is the answer—the kingdom has come. The Church is jubilant. They worship Adoni-Elohim-Shaddai, the One "who art and wast" (not "will be," for He has arrived).

(4) *The nations were angry (wroth)* reveals the stubborn rebellion of man right down to the very last—even trying to shut Him out when He finally comes to this world, for His coming interferes with their plans. They are angry because the power is to be taken out of their hands.

Why do the heathen rage, and the people imagine a vain [empty] thing? (Psalm 2:1).

If today Christ should come to the heads of government suggesting that they retire for He had come to take over, what do you think the reaction would be? Would they welcome Him? Would Russia welcome Him? Would Great Britain welcome Him? Would the United States of America welcome Him? When Christ does come, man will not surrender. He must be defeated. Man would dethrone God if he could. Man resists to the end and declares war against God. God will meet the attack. That is the reason it says in the second Psalm that He will break them with a rod of iron—He has to.

Then shall the LORD go forth, and fight against those nations, as when he fought in the day of battle (Zechariah 14:3).

Antichrist marches against God (see Daniel 11:36).

Who opposeth and exalteth himself above all that is called God, or that is worshipped; so that he as God sitteth in the temple of God, showing himself that he is God (II Thessalonians 2:4).

Today the natural man resents any suggestion that he surrender to God; but it is our glorious privilege, in this day of His rejection, to yield to Him, to accept Him, to say with Thomas, "My Lord and my God."

(5) *And thy wrath came* is a strange statement for this generation which has been weaned on the saccharine sweetness of a watered-down "love of God," and has been brainwashed by a false theology of sweetness and light—which minimizes the sin of man and the holiness and righteousness of God. Today "there is no fear of God before their eyes." Most people believe that God is incapable of anger. The long day of God's mercy and grace, in which He has moved with patience, has contributed to the formulation of this false philosophy. The men of our day need to take another look at Romans 1:18:

For the wrath of God is revealed from heaven against all ungodliness and unrighteousness of men, who hold the truth in unrighteousness;

A day of wrath is coming (see Zephaniah 1:15, 16; Isaiah 13:9).

But after thy hardness and impenitent heart treasurest up unto thyself wrath against the day of wrath and revelation of the righteous judgment of God (Romans 2:5).

These are but a few of the Scriptures which speak of the day of God's wrath.

(6) *And the time of the dead to be judged* brings us to the Great White Throne judgment of the lost dead (see Revelation 20:11-15).

(7) *And to give the reward to your servants the prophets, and to the saints, and to them that fear thy name, the small and the great.* The rapture of the Church has taken place previously (Revelation 4:4), and the believers already have been rewarded, as indicated by the crowns on the heads of the elders. Hence this refers, we believe, not to the Church, but to the Old Testament prophets, and all of God's own in the Old Testament, and the Tribulation saints both small and great. It is at this time, when Christ returns to the earth and the Millennium begins, that the Old Testament and Tribulation saints are to be raised and rewarded for entrance into the Millennial Kingdom.

(8) *And to destroy those who destroy (corrupt, the destroyers of) the earth* refers, we believe, to both man and Satan. Man is a destroyer:

Destruction and misery are in their ways (Romans 3:16).

Satan is a destroyer of man:

> In whom the god of this world hath blinded the minds of them which believe not, lest the light of the glorious gospel of Christ, who is the image of God, should shine unto them (II Corinthians 4:4).

Peter warns us of Satan:

> Be sober, be vigilant; because your adversary the devil, as a roaring lion, walketh about, seeking whom he may devour (I Peter 5:8).

This is the final end of all evil. It will not break out again in rebellion in all of creation (see I Corinthians 15:26-28; Revelation 20:7-10). The walls of Jericho have at last fallen down. The nations were angry, but there was and is joy in heaven.

This brings us to the glad gate of eternity.

Verse 19—And the temple of God was opened in heaven, and there was seen in his temple the ark of his testament: and there were lightnings, and voices and thunderings, and an earthquake, and great hail.

And the sanctuary (temple) of God in heaven was opened, and the ark of His covenant was seen in His sanctuary (temple), and there followed lightnings, and voices, and thunders, and an earthquake, and great hail.

Sanctuary (temple) of God in heaven confirms again that there is a literal temple in heaven (see Exodus 25:40; Hebrews 8:2-5; 9:23, 24).

Was opened indicates worship and access to God. All of this points to the nation Israel—the Church has no temple (see Revelation 21:22). The measuring of the temple on earth and the opening of the temple in heaven declares the prominence of Israel in this section. The next chapter substantiates this.

And the ark of His covenant was seen in His sanctuary reminds us that we are dealing with a covenant-making and covenant-keeping God. He will keep the covenants He has made with Israel and He will make a new covenant with them at this time (see Jeremiah 31:31-34; Hebrews 8:8-13).

> For this is my covenant unto them, when I shall take away their sins (Romans 11:27).

One of the apocryphal books (II Maccabees) tells about Jeremiah hiding the ark when Nebuchadnezzar took the city of Jerusalem. Tradition has it that it is hidden away in Ethiopia and will be brought out some day. This is, of course, speculation. Jeremiah dismisses the ark for the future:

> And it shall come to pass, when ye be multiplied and increased in the land, in those days, saith the LORD, they shall say no more, The ark of the covenant of the LORD: neither shall it come to mind: neither shall they remember it; neither shall they visit it; neither shall that be done any more (Jeremiah 3:16).

The ark, mentioned in this last verse of chapter 11, is not the ark of the Old Testament. Govett has well said, "God has a better ark and a better covenant in store for His people Israel."

Lightnings, and voices, and thunders, and an earthquake, and great hail speak of judgment yet to come. The time is short but the Great Tribulation has not ended. The voices indicate that it is moving not in a haphazard way, but with intelligence. Vincent calls them, "the solemn salvos, so to speak, of the artillery of heaven, with which each series of visions is concluded."

BIBLIOGRAPHY

RECOMMENDED BOOKS

Govett, Robert. *The Apocalypse Expounded by Scripture.* London: Thyme, 1922.

Ironside, H.A. *Lectures on the Book of Revelation.* Neptune, New Jersey: Loizeaux, 1960.

Lindsay, Hal. *There's a New World Coming.* Santa Ana, California: Vision House Publishers, 1973.

Newell, William R. *The Book of Revelation.* Chicago: Moody Press, 1935.

Ryrie, Charles C. *Revelation.* Chicago: Moody Press, 1968. (A fine, inexpensive survey of the book.)

Scott, Walter. *Exposition of the Revelation of Jesus Christ.* London: Pickering and Inglis, n.d.

Seiss, J.A. *The Apocalypse, Lectures on the Book of Revelation.* Grand Rapids: Zondervan, 1957.

Smith, J.B. *A Revelation of Jesus Christ.* Scottsdale, Pennsylvania: Herald Press, 1961.

Strauss, Lehman. *The Book of Revelation.* Neptune, New Jersey: Loizeaux, 1964.

Walvoord, John F. *The Revelation of Jesus Christ.* Chicago: Moody Press, 1966.

HELPFUL BOOKS ON BIBLE PROPHECY

Hoyt, Herman A. *The End Times.* Chicago: Moody Press, 1969.

Pentecost, J. Dwight. *Things to Come.* Grand Rapids: Dunham, 1958.

Pentecost, J. Dwight. *Prophecy For Today.* Grand Rapids: Zondervan, 1961.

Pentecost, J. Dwight, *Will Man Survive?* Chicago: Moody Press, 1971.

Ryrie, Charles C. *The Basis of the Premillennial Faith.* Neptune, New Jersey: Loizeaux, 1953.

Ryrie, Charles C. *The Bible and Tomorrow's News.* Wheaton, Illinois: Scripture Press Publications, 1969.

Unger, Merrill F. *Beyond the Crystal Ball.* Chicago: Moody Press, 1973.

Walvoord, John F. *Armageddon, Oil and the Middle East Crisis.* Grand Rapids: Zondervan, 1974.

Walvoord, John F. *The Blessed Hope and the Tribulation.* Grand Rapids: Zondervan, 1976.

Walvoord, John F. *The Millennial Kingdom.* Grand Rapids: Dunham, 1959.

Thru The Bible Books

P. O. Box 100   •   Pasadena, California 91109